A Tapestry of Treachery

An Amarna Tragedy-The Life and Death

of Rib-Hadda of Sumur

By

Rick Baude

Email. barricademan@gmail.com

Table of Contents

Page

1

Preface

Confessions of an Amarnaholic

I've been an unwitting fan of Amarna virtually my whole life. It all started, innocently enough, decades ago in the flower of my youth when I was a kid and saw the first pictures of Tutankhamen's golden funerary mask. It was staggering; mind-blowing. At first, I thought Tutankhamen was one of the powerhouses of Egyptian history. Clearly, he was a man who must have walked across the landscape in seven-league boots gazing down on everybody cowering beneath him. Obviously, he must have been on par with Alexander the Great, Genghis Khan or Atilla the Hun in order to deserve such a magnificent burial. And then the truth wandered into the room like a shabbily dressed itinerant truth teller from a Homeric story. You know the buzz killers I'm talking about? They're the ones who walk into a banquet room filled with drunken revelers at the height of the party, and delivers the news that they will all die a horrible death, ironically by their own hand, before the night ends. At first, they don't believe her, but then as their fingers grow numb, and their speech begins to slur they realize, too late, that the prophecy has come true. They indeed have died by their own hand; after they drank the poisoned wine served to them by their gracious host.

However, as my studies advanced, I discovered that in reality Tutankhamen was a rather insignificant ruler of the 18th dynasty. We didn't know much about him before the discovery of his tomb, and now almost a hundred years later we don't know much more than the fact that he lived and died.

As far as royal burials went his tomb was actually a bargain basement affair. Originally it had been carved for someone else, perhaps a noble, but it had quickly and expeditiously been repurposed when King Tut died unexpectedly. In fact, much of the funeral equipment, including his famous gold mask, had been recycled from other royal burials.

But that didn't matter to me I was hooked. As the years and decades passed, I read intermittently, (and unsystematically) a substantial amount of the material on Amarna. This was of course back in the dark ages long before the internet and before Amazon.com made it easy to buy any book on any subject that you wanted and have it delivered to your doorstep in a couple of days. In those dark ages, libraries had a few books on Tutankhamen and not much else. Bookstores would sell the bestsellers and that was it. Access to the basic literature and journals was locked up in university libraries and so my Amarna studies were limited and confined to the popular literature.

And then the internet became available to the general public. After that it was just like the sun rising over the horizon showing areas that I never knew existed. I now had access to a vast array of literature and ideas. It was here that I entered into many heated discussions with various people on different web-sites about Amarna. Then I slowly realized I was completely transfixed with Amarna and everything Amarna as I tried to unravel the secrets of this fascinating period of Egyptian history. Finally, I realized that I had come more or less come to the end of the road of Amarna studies. After all, how many times can you look at the same photographs? Or read the same descriptions of Tut's tomb before you realize that you were just running in circles. It was time to leave Amarna. As a result, I set myself up as the president of a self-help group dedicated to trying to extricate ourselves from the 'Amarna Tar Pits' as I humorously called them. I named the group "Amarnaholics Anonymous". I was the self-appointed president, chief therapist, and sole member of the group and I candidly admit that I've fallen off the wagon so many times that I finally just let the wagon and its driver continue on their lonely journey without me. Instead, I have continued on my journey through Amarna. Evidently the road to redemption and salvation isn't one that I was meant to follow. Needless to say, I've been an abject failure at separating myself from Amarna.

So, as part of the healing process, I decided to write about my explorations and discoveries in Amarna, in particular the 'Amarna Letters'. Originally, I had planned this as a scholarly book. But then as I started researching and writing it, and thought about it I realized I was in over my head.

Why you might ask?

Alas that isn't my skill set. As a result, I quickly took a couple of aspirin and laid down for several hours while I watched some Star Trek episodes. Then as I slowly sobered up from that fever dream, I returned to composing a far easier to write, and read, straight narrative historical work.

So, why exactly did I abandon an academic work? Well to start with writing an academic book requires armies of footnotes marching across the bottom of each page like loyal soldiers amplifying something that you already said in the body of the text. In addition to that you need notes referencing other author's works. And that's just the beginning of this magnificent odyssey. Ideally, you should have access to the source material. You must be able to read ancient, and living languages with equal ease and have unfettered access to the main players in the field. You should also have multiple other skill sets that I don't have, and at this point in my life I have no interest in acquiring. And finally, you should have a bibliography that references every book you touched, looked at, or thought about during the course of your research. As the current transportation idioms go "This is out of my wheelhouse" and as a result "I'll stay in my own lane."

Instead, I bravely faced reality and now armed with a renewed sense of purpose, I decided to write an all-purpose, one-size-fits all non-scholastic narrative history of Amarna. An accessible book that would serve as a gateway book to future Amarnaphiles, as I describe my discoveries while wandering through the Amarna Hall of Mirrors.

What follows is a result of my journeys as an armchair historian.

Chapter 1

All Egyptology is Divided into Three Periods

Whenever I survey the books on Egyptology that are for sale it seems that most of them cover three distinct periods of the subject. The first category invariably has pictures of the sun rising over (or setting behind) the great pyramid of Egypt (with the sphinx either absent from the picture, and if present either in the foreground or the background). This falls into a category that Egyptologists call the Old Kingdom. The second category has photos of Tutankhamen's funeral mask, or golden coffin, or the world famous bust of Nefertiti. This period is known as the "Middle Kingdom" and then finally the third category deals with the last queen of Egypt; Cleopatra. This is unsurprisingly called "The New Kingdom". All three kingdoms are interspersed with three time periods when Egypt collapsed for various reasons they are called "The First Intermediate" period, "The Second Intermediate period" and (big drumroll) "The Third Intermediate period".

When I see these books I think of Julius Caesar's famous description of ancient Britain, that "All Gaul can be divided into three parts." Only instead I'll modify to it to read "All Egyptology can be divided into three parts; 1) The Great Pyramids, 2) Amarna, and 3) Cleopatra". Of course, like all sweeping generalizations there are a boatload of exceptions to the rule. And sprinkled, among the big three categories, like soggy croutons on a wilting salad, are a potpourri of new age books dealing with pyramid power, the secrets of the sphinx, Edgar Cayce books and space aliens. These fall into a category derisively referred to as Pyramidiots. And finally, there are an assortment of novels, coloring books, puzzles and games all with an Egyptology theme to them.

Ah yes, I can hear the rumbling in the background as professional Egyptologists and scholars muttering *en masse* at this continent-sized sweeping generalization. "Really?" they might say with an edge in their collective voices. "What about Narmer who united Upper and Lower Egypt? You know the guy whose cosmetic pallet had him inspecting ten headless corpses? Did you forget Djoser the pharaoh who built the step pyramid (BTW his pyramid is in my opinion the most fascinating of them that would be the model for the pyramids that followed?) What about Queen Hatshepsut who wrestled the crown from her nephew's hands and literally ruled in name as a king, and not a queen? Did you forget Ramses the Great? How about Ptolemy the founder of the longest dynasty in history?" And, of course, I would instantly and unhesitatingly agree with them. Yes, yes in fact there is more to Egyptology than these three subjects.

Instead, in this book I will focus exclusively on perhaps one of the most lackluster and mundane aspects of Amarna studies; a group of clay tablets known collectively as the "Amarna Letters".

What are the 'Amarna Letters'? Well briefly, they're a collection of clay tablets that were discovered in Egypt at the end of the 19th century. They basically fall into two broad categories. The first category are letters written to the various kings in the middle east while the second category consists of letters that were written to and from the King's vassals, both categories take place during this time period,

Even though they are short, fragmented, repetitive, and at times boring, they are still unique in that they give us a deep insight into an aspect of Egyptian history that has been previously hidden to us.

Chapter 2

Foot mail, Clay mail, Snail mail, and E-mail

Since the Amarna letters are about communication, I think we should do a quick review of communication methods throughout history.

The earliest method of long-range message transmission was undoubtedly what we would call 'foot mail'. What happened was a ruler would dictate his message to a carrier who would run at top speed to the neighboring kingdom where he would recite verbatim ruler 1's message to ruler 2. Ruler 2 in turn would then dictate a return message to the first king. This would continue until everything was either settled to everybody's satisfaction or they went to war.

In today's digital era we have various types of 'mail'. For instance, if you leave a message on an answering machine it's called 'voice mail'. But if you send a digital letter, you've sent an 'e-mail'. On the other hand, if you send a physical letter through the mail system, that's 'snail mail' since it moves at the speed of the various delivery vehicles.

And finally, there is 'clay mail'. 'What is clay mail?' Well, it's one of the most enduring systems of recording information ever invented. It appears to be about 5,000 years old and started in the middle east when some genius or group of geniuses invented writing. And after that they began writing on clay tablets. This highly efficient method of communication caught on quickly and before long virtually all communications were taking place via clay mail. It was then adopted by different cultures in the middle east for millennia. There are literally thousands of documents of all types and eras that have been translated or await translation.

In the ancient middle east, there were various kingdoms always rising and falling. They would break away from one empire, and start their own empire, or be absorbed into another existing one. There were trade and diplomatic matters that had to addressed and the problem was how to make sure everybody was speaking the same language. Even though we don't know the exact method that took place, with multiple unrelated languages being spoken throughout the near east it was essential to find a *lingua franca* for trade and diplomacy. Even, though they spoke different languages everybody finally settled on the written language known as Akkadian, as the language of diplomacy and trade.

As such the Amarna Letters fall solidly in the "Clay Mail" category of communication. So, what exactly are the "Amarna Letters"? Well, like the name implies, they're a collection of letters inscribed on clay tablets written in the wedge-shaped cuneiform writing using the Akkadian language to send messages to the various kings and vassals in the Levant from Egypt.

The standard dogma is that the letters were discovered by a woman who was digging to find soil that could be used for farming in the abandoned city of Akhet-Aten. After that they made their way into the antiquities market and from there, they entered various museums and private collections around the world, and then into the scholastic world, and from there into this book and finally into your hands.

However, after researching deeper, I began to have my doubts about the veracity of this story. It all sounded to contrived for my skeptical mind. And then I had my doubts confirmed. As I dug deeper into the history and translation of the tablets, I found this quote from an earlier source about the discovery of the tablets *"In the beginning of 1888 some fellahin digging for marl not far from the ruins came upon a number of crumbling wooden chests, filled with clay tablets closely covered on both sides with writing. The dusky fellows must have been not a little delighted at finding themselves owners of hundreds of these marketable tablets."*

A number of things came screaming out of this introduction, in no particular order they are; 1) The initial discoverers were actually a group of men 2) They weren't fellahin innocently digging for soil, but were in fact organized thieves who used 'digging for soil' as a cover story for their theft. 3) They instantly recognized the value of what they had found. 4) and they knew that European collectors would pay a hefty price in gold for them. 5) Once the tablets entered the international black market the governments of Britain and Egypt quickly got wind of the discovery and slammed the brakes on the enterprise 6) and as a result most of the Amarna tablets promptly left Egypt and wound up in the hands of European museums with the most pristine ones landing in the British Museum.

This did not strike me as a lucky discovery. No, it was obvious that this was part of an organized group of professional thieves and international art dealers. They knew what to look for, where to search for it, how to move it quickly onto the black market and after that get the goods out of the country before it was too late. Finally in order to cover their tracks the gang of male thieves looting an archeological site, was magically transformed into a naive peasant woman innocently looking for soil in which to grow her vegetables.

Since clay tablets written in Akkadian using the cuneiform had never been found in Egypt, before, they were at first considered frauds. But before long they were recognized as authentic.

Once the "Amarna Letters" were translated scholars found that they dealt with a variety of subjects. One group was primarily diplomatic correspondence between the various great powers at the time and the other larger group were from the various vassals in the Northern Levant who answered to the Egyptian pharaoh.

However, as small and fragmentary as they are they still give us a window into the machinations of the Egyptian empire under the reign of three pharaohs Amenhotep III, Akhenaten, Smenkhare and possibly Tutankhamen.

Even though it is a relatively small collection, the entire corpus of letters covers a time range that is not very long (about 30 years by some estimates) and consists of about 350 letters.

However, even that is too large to evaluate in one book and as such virtually all studies of the Amarna letters are confined to a handful of them at most. So, following in that tradition I'll zero in on a subset of the Amarna letters that were written by an inconsequential Egyptian vassal who lived and died in the Northern Levant in an area that is now located around modern-day Beirut. The man's name was Rib-Hadda.

Chapter 3

And Now a Man Who Needs an Introduction;

Rib-Hadda of Sumur

Since Rib-Hadda is the main character of this book we'll need to spend some time collecting the fragmentary information about him and try and use it to reconstruct his life.

To start with who was he? What did he look like? What did he do? Unfortunately, he has left us with no image to gaze upon; nor are there any statues dedicated to him. Unlike the kings and nobility of his time there is no tomb to mark where he was buried, or paintings of the man to gaze upon, or stela to boast about the things that he accomplished in life. Alas the man has vanished into the dust from which he rose.

In fact, the only reason we know Rib-Hadda existed at all is because of a handful of letters that he wrote to the Egyptian pharaoh and to other people in the Egyptian bureaucracy.

Rib-Hadda's correspondence itself consists of about 70 letters and from this meager source we'll have to reconstruct his life. In his letters, Rib-Hadda complains endlessly about everything. To hear him tell it nothing works, everybody is out to get him, he is surrounded by enemies, his cities are falling like dominos in an earthquake, he has no provisions etc. Amazingly even with this never-ending litany of complaints and escalating problems, he still swears a Job-like undying loyalty to the Pharaoh. And what does the pharaoh do in return? Well, the Pharaoh repays Rib-Haddas loyalty by ignoring his requests for aid and supplies and in general just lets Rib-Hadda twist slowly in the desert wind.   After a while one gets the feeling that Rib-Hadda might as well have dropped his letters down the nearest well, for all the good that they did.

Chapter 4

The Three Empires Problem

In order to understand Rib-Hadda's plight we have to locate him in both time and space. We know that he lived 3500 years ago, in the city of Sumur which was located in present day Northern Lebanon. Geographically, he was surrounded by three empires; the Hittites were to the north, in what is now modern-day Turkey, the Mitannians to the west in what is generally Syria, and the Egyptians in Northern Africa. In other words, Rib-Hadda was right at the very junction of where these three empires collided.

But his problems only worsen; 'Hatti', the country which was the home of the Hittites, was now under the dynamic leader of a King Suppiluliumas. After Suppiluliumas had finished consolidating his power at home, he began flexing his military muscles by making a series of incursions into the region controlled by the Mitannians. It was apparent that the Hittites were on the move and weren't going to stop until they had become the dominant power in the Northern Levant.

On the other hand, the Mitannian empire which had, up until that time, been one of the region's superpowers was beginning to eclipse and crumble. The Mitannian empire, at that time was headed by King Tusratta.

History shows that there was a two-prong pincher attack of their empire; on one side they had the Hittites pressing up against them. While on the other side Assyria, (which had been one of Mitanni's former client states) was now shaking itself loose from Mitannian dominance and beginning its ascent on the world stage.

Egypt, now headed by Akhenaten, which had formerly, been a strong Mitannian ally, was now for unknown reasons, strangely ambivalent to Mitanni's downward spiral and did nothing when it was finally crushed by the Hittite juggernaut.

Unsurprisingly, Rib-Hadda was at the very epicenter of the political earthquake that was shaking this part of the world.

The next question is what was Rib-Hadda's position in the Egyptian hierarchy? Well, in the literature he has been called a 'mayor', or a 'governor' of the cities over which he had authority; but in my opinion 'mayor' and 'governor' are pretty much modern-day terms that really don't describe Rib-Hadda's position in the Egyptian government. The one thing that clashes with the use of 'mayor' is that currently the mayor is the elected urban leader of a single city. They usually confine themselves to problems such as trash pick-up, fixing pot holes in the street, and making sure the city operates on a day-to-day basis. The position is elective and both men and women can hold the position.

However, in the Amarna letters the 'mayor' is always a man, he can control a single city or as many as he can seize. In addition to that he could hunt down other mayors and kill them, enlist mercenaries to achieve his end, and evidently, he had his own private army. Not only that but he would blockade harbors, cut off the food and water supply of other cities, and make alliances with foreign entities.

The position was apparently achieved in one of three ways. 1) They inherited it from a male relative. 2) They seized the position by killing another mayor who was already in power. 3) They conquered another city and then killed the mayor and took over. 4) Or least likely, they were appointed by the Pharaoh.

The mayors themselves answered to a variety of commissioners who were all appointed by the Pharaoh. From what I can see mayors, were never promoted to commissioners, and commissioners were never demoted to mayors. If an organization chart was created, the mayors would be nominally subordinate to the commissioners, supposedly doing what they were told to do, when they were told to do it. The reality is that even though the mayors made the obligatory promises of obeying every word that the king had written. It's also abundantly clear that they did whatever the hell they wanted to do, or had to do, in order to survive, or achieve their own ends.

The evidence is also overwhelming from the Amarna Letters that because of the distances involved, the commissioners' power was diluted, which allowed the mayors to only pay lip service to the orders they received. The evidence is also abundant that if a commissioner did get too nosey, or aggressive they could end up with a knife in their back and their body dumped somewhere in the desert for the jackals to feed on. As a result, one gets the impression that the wisest commissioners spent their time reading letters from the vassals and passing on the information in letters to the pharaoh, and not micro-managing the affairs of their subordinates.

Chapter 5

A Name What's in a Name?

One of the main problems that people have with their first encounter with the Amarna Letters is that virtually all of the names in the corpus sound like they're characters out of a Star Wars movie. Only instead of Padmé Amidala Naberrie (The queen of Naboodie) or Beru Whitesun Lars (Luke Skywalker's surrogate mother) or Kanan Jarrus (A Jedi survivor). We get a cast of real-life characters with names like Yanhamu, Abdi Asirta, and Panhamata just to name a few from a cast of hundreds.

Another problem with the Amarna letters is that you feel like you are walking into the middle of a movie that was assembled by a drunken film editor; the end is at the beginning, the beginning is missing entirely, major characters have vanished, some of the film is upside down while other parts of the film are playing backwards and then somehow or another, we the audience have to decipher what the movie is all about.

This especially holds true for Rib-Hadda. When we first meet him there is no introduction as to who he is, or what his position is within the Egyptian empire, nor do we know how long he has held it. In various popular works he's referred to as a 'prince', 'governor' or 'mayor'. But these terms fall far short of describing his position. The evidence shows he clearly didn't have the power of a prince, nor was he royalty of any kind, but he was far more powerful than any contemporary mayor. Based, on the meager internal evidence we do know that he answers to a commissioner named Panhamata, who at that time was providing him with supplies. And after that he asked to be placed another commissioner named Yanhamu. As we'll discover that was disastrous request for Rib-Hadda.

In fact, the problem of locating Rib-Hadda's position in the Egyptian hierarchy is that he never tells us what his title is! This is in contradistinction to most Egyptian monuments where titles are dropped like leaves falling off a tree in Autumn. Interestingly the few times that he does refer to himself it's almost always with some debasing description like the 'dust beneath the king's feet', and in one case as the King's 'footstool'; these are hardly titles that one would aspire to! Even though this sounds like nauseating groveling to us these are rather common descriptions used throughout the Amarna letters.

The first clue as to Rib-Hadda's position in government might lie in Rib-Hadda's name itself. After scouring the late Dr. Youngblood's unpublished doctoral thesis. I discovered it's a treasure trove of information that, is apparently well known to Biblical scholars, but is virtually unknown to the general public and as such it unlocks some of the secrets of the Amarna archive.

According to Dr. Youngblood, Rib-Hadda's name means "The Compensation of Hadad" which indicates the previous loss of a brother. 'Haddad', continuing to follow Youngblood, was actually the name of a Cannanite storm god. Drawing these clues together then the evidence is that Rib-Hadda inherited his position as 'mayor' and wasn't appointed to it by Akhenaten or any previous pharaoh.

It's also difficult to locate Abdi-Asirta's position in the government, which makes his relationship to Rib-Hadda equally difficult to ascertain.

Except for always calling him "the traitorous dog" we also never find out what Abdi-Asirta's true title is. The fact that they both answer to a 'commissioner' strongly suggests that the two men held equivalent ranks.

Other clues about Rib-Hadda's status emerge tangentially from other fields. For instance, when we turn to the study of 'paleography', the field that compares various writing techniques in order to decide who actually wrote a document, and when it was written, a different picture emerges. In this case after doing a paleographic study of the tablets one scholar has concluded that two different scribes wrote some of the letters that Rib-Hadda had sent them to the king. This in itself is a valuable clue. Why? Because we know from other sources that scribes were at the top of the employment pyramid, and the fact that Rib-Hadda had two of them means he must have had considerable means to keep them on the payroll.

It's also interesting that from time-to-time Rib-Hadda apparently bypasses his boss in the chain of command and appeals directly to the Pharaoh who as usual ignores him.

What ultimately happened to Rib-Hadda? Well, unsurprisingly, in the time-honored tradition of middle eastern politics he was eventually assassinated. After his death Rib-Hadda's brother apparently took control of the territory that had formerly been entrusted to Rib-Hadda. Subsequently Rib-Hadda was forgotten about for almost 3500 years; only to reenter the historical record when his letters were discovered and translated in the 19th century. In the end it was obvious that in the middle-east eco-system Rib-Hadda lived in, he was at or near the bottom, of the bureaucratic food chain.

Now after having read this brief biography, I imagine you're drumming your fingers impatiently asking the question "Okay Rick so why exactly would you devote an entire book to an inconsequential nobody? Why, oh why are you giving us this twenty-one-gun salute to mediocrity by writing this tome about a historical non-entity?" A person that even professional Egyptologists mention only in passing or cover briefly? Well, the primary reason is that even though the lion's share of the media attention goes to Akhenaten, Nefertiti and Tutankhamen, (and as fascinating as they were), it's important to keep in mind that they weren't the only players on the field. No, in order to keep the music and festivities and the perpetual motion party machine that was going on at Amarna there was a whole bureaucratic and economic machine in place supporting and maintaining them. As such we have to keep in mind that millions of people lived and died under the Pharaohs and that with the exception of a few fragments here and there we know nothing about them. But by studying the Amarna letters in general and Rib-Hadda in particular we can begin to piece together a picture of what the lower half lived like and from there get an overall portrait of ancient times.

Chapter 6

A Portrait of the Pharaoh as a Self-indulgent Tyrant,

or Fast Times at Akhet-Aten

Before we take a deep dive into Rib-Hadda's life we first need to get an overview of the world in which he lived and take a whirlwind tour of the latter part of the 18th dynasty.

Unlike Rib-Hadda who left us only a handful of clay tablets to document his existence. King Akhenaten, Tutankhamen, and Queen Nefertiti, along with a host of other Amarna figures, left us with an abundant supply of cities, temples, tombs, statues, coffins, mummies, and wall murals to study.

In fact, there's so much material that we even know what they ate for dinner (duck). In addition to that we pretty much know what went on in their public and private lives as well. And now with further advances in DNA technology we know their exact relationship to each other.

First, let's turn our attention to Akhenaten.

Akhenaten didn't start out as Akhenaten, but rather as Amenhotep IVth. He was the latest pharaoh in a series of kings that had successfully expelled the invading Hyksos in the 17th dynasty that had then given rise to the "Thuthmosid" dynasty that expanded the borders of the Egyptian empire. Now, with the country solidly united it grew and prospered. Everything was just fine until one day the Pharaoh Amenhotep III died and "spread his wings from horizon to horizon and flew to the west" to use that exquisite Egyptian euphemism for death. After that he was safely tucked away in his 'house of eternity', as his tomb was known, in the Valley of the Kings.

With the death of Amenhotep III naturally his son, Amenhotep IV, ascended the throne and took his place as head of the army, the government and the theocracy. At first Amenhotep IV's future reign didn't seem particularly promising or auspicious. Up until that point in time the only mention of him is from a single wine docket. However, in view of the ensuing turbulent history that would follow it's difficult to imagine a more inauspicious beginning than that.

But if the past is any indicator of the future, then the country should have continued harmoniously as it had for over a thousand years before that, following the natural rhythm of the Nile and its harvesting season, while diplomacy would be carried out on the international front and the gods would be worshipped as they had for millennia before. Unfortunately, in this case the past was a predictor of absolutely nothing, especially concerning the revolution that the young king was about to introduce. No, in fact, from our perspective, almost everything changed overnight.

At the time the chief god in the Egyptian pantheon was "Amun" which meant "The Hidden One". Amun himself presided over a vast array of gods and goddess (far too many to be mentioned much less described in detail) who were part of an ancient, rich and deep spiritual tradition.

The problem was that shortly after Amenhotep IV took power a religious crisis erupted. It seemed that the young pharaoh had conceived of a completely new and revolutionary religious order. In this novel theology there was only one God; the sun god Aten, and his manifestation was the physical sun. Of course, new gods had appeared before in Egyptian history and they were assimilated into the easy-going religion of the Ancient Egyptians.

But there were some critical differences; the 'Aten' was not a new god but an aspect of the sun god that went back at least to the ancient pyramids, and perhaps beyond that. It's important to realize that this was not the rise of a god that already existed within the pantheon. Actually, this was the obliteration of that pantheon along with all of its texts, and practices including temples that had been open for millennia. Going forward there would be no other gods or goddesses other than the Aten.

Unsurprisingly with this radical departure from orthodoxy a struggle broke out between Amenhotep IV and the priests of Amun over which god would be paramount in Egyptian society. The question was who would prevail? Would it be either the ancient cult of Amun 'the hidden one' or would it be the pharaoh's new solar cult with its sole reigning god of the Aten' that would rule over Egypt?

What exactly happened during this theological tempest in a teapot is impossible to tell. Unfortunately, what's left of the record is so fragmentary and distorted that we can only make hesitant guesses about what was going on behind the scenes. The one thing that we do know is that this theological battle went on for five years and when it was over the king finally emerged more or less triumphant.

After the theological dust settled, the temples were closed and the old god 'Amun' was out along with the entire Egyptian pantheon of Osiris, Neith, Seth, Isis, Horus and hundreds of other minor gods and goddesses also vanished with him. In the end the 'Aten' ruled supreme and alone. And there was one final casualty to the list; the king's name. Somewhere during this time Amenhotep IV'th was transformed into Akhenaten.

But there were still more tempestuous changes to be made. Apparently, Akhenaten found Thebes to be a festering cesspool of theological turbulence in which it was impossible to reside anymore. So, the king pulled up stakes from the ancient city and began looking for a place in Egypt to build a new capital. According to the surviving evidence engraved on the boundary stela at Akhet-Aten, he searched for an area that had never been claimed by man or God or goddess. Finally, after months of searching on the dusty plains of Egypt he found the place where he would build his city of the sun.

After that he moved the entire capital from Thebes to a desolate spot in the desert where a new city was built from the ground up. A city he called Akhet-Aten "The Horizon of the Sun".

Akhet-Aten emerged like a beautiful flower after a rainstorm. From the surviving decorations in the various nobles' tombs, we know that there was dancing and music being played as the ultra-rich and powerful basked in the presence of the Pharaoh and his entourage. For them life was a perpetual motion party that never ended. But like all things in life, the never ending party and endless sacrifices to the Aten ended with the death of Akhenaten.

After Akhenaten's death the history becomes murky and the exact sequence of events becomes opaque. He was probably succeeded by "Nefertiti" (the reason I put Nefertiti in quotes is because there were two Nefertiti's at Akhet-Aten; Nefertiti the queen and wife of Akhenaten, and one of her daughters also named Nefertiti, but which Nefertiti took power is still unresolved). However, after she died, it appears that the ephemeral Smenkhare assumed the throne for a year or two (at the most) before he too died. Finally, after their deaths, Tutankh*aten* assumes the throne at the age of 9, instantly changed his name to Tutankh*amen* and promptly moved the capital back to Thebes. The now abandoned Akhet-Aten slowly returned to the desert from which it had arisen.

Years after the city was evacuated it was razed (probably by Horemhab who destroyed it and used the rubble as fill for the various pylons in some temples construction) and forgotten about for the next 3500 years. It was only in the 19th century when the city was rediscovered and its fragmentary history pieced together that its importance in history became apparent.

But these aren't the only questions that pervade this era. Among others is the question of did a co-regency exist? We know for a fact that co-regencies existed throughout Egyptian history. So naturally the question arises if there was a co-regency between Akhenaten and someone else. Was there a long co-regency of maybe thirty years? Or was there a short co-regency of maybe five years? Or maybe there was no co-regency at all and it's just another reflection in the Amarna Hall of Mirrors. For me the Amarna co-regency is like a soccer ball at a brilliantly played soccer game i.e., the ball keeps switching sides but for various reasons neither team can keep possession of the ball or win the game.

As far as my opinion about the co-regency problem, I'll just say that at one time I was an active and vociferous participant in the co-regency debate. But over the decades I have since morphed and mellowed into a bemused spectator with no particular opinion on the matter but I lean very strongly to the 'no coregency' side. As such I've seen proposals for a co-regency between Akhenaten and his father Amenhotep III? Perhaps his mother Tiye? Maybe there was one with his wife Nefertiti? Or perhaps the putative co-regent was Tutankhamen. On the other hand, perhaps it's the frequently mentioned but never seen Smenkhare who is the co-regent? Then again maybe he ruled alone and the alleged co-regency is just another Amarna mirage; a product of wishful thinking and scholarship that is based solidly on the shaky foundation of confirmational bias rather than unbiased and objective facts.

Other questions that remain to be answered definitively, are who is the anonymous male mummy who was buried in a woman's coffin in KV 55? Was it the great heretic Akhenaten himself? Or was it perhaps Akhenaten's immediate successor, the ever-elusive Smenkhare? And then again maybe it was somebody else entirely? Unfortunately, the only thing we can say with certainty is "Who knows?"

Another question that's never been answered is where is Queen/King Nefertiti buried? After all her power was undisputed in the surviving fragments of Amarna history, so surely, she had her own tomb. But if she did where is it? In the Valley of the Kings or somewhere else? Maybe it was back at Akhet-Aten? Or perhaps it was someplace else entirely? So far nobody knows.

The Amarna "Hall of Mirrors "is utterly captivating and equally baffling.

In closing this section, it should be mentioned that the exact sequence of events is still hotly contested. As such this description is nothing more than the barest of bare bones assessment of the history of the city of Akhet-Aten and the succession sequence in Akhenaten.

Chapter 7

Abandon all Hope Ye Who Enter Here

On the surface Amarna looks like a perpetual motion song and dance festival with everybody living the high life presided over by the loving and benign Akhenaten accompanied by his gorgeous wife Nefertiti and presided over by his sole god the Aten.

However, when we zoom in for a closer look at the dynasty, we find that things aren't quite as rosy as they appear. Our first clues come from some of the surviving monuments. One such monument shows servants bowing before Nefertiti as she walks forward and another set of servants, also bowing, who are following her. At every point in the decorative scenes, we see servants groveling at Akhenaten's and Nefertiti's feet with every step they took.

One gets the uneasy feeling that absolute servility and devotion to the king seem to be the passport to success at Akhet-Aten.

In many versions of the Amarna mythology Akhenaten is portrayed as a pacifist. A peace-loving soul who is lost in contemplation of the Aten. However, this is contradicted by the artwork. Akhenaten is seen in various friezes being escorted to his palace by his army! This depiction as far as I know is unique in Egyptian art. Above them in the sky the Aten's beneficent rays are shining down exclusively on Akhenaten and the royal family. Finally, in a rare instance we see the usually aloof and passive Nefertiti energetically bashing a Nubian prisoners' brains out with a club.

When we turn to the surviving hymns and prayers to the Aten, we find that they are surprisingly shallow and free of any deep or meaningful philosophy. They babble on with self-evident inanities about the sun shining down on everybody, and giving life to everything on earth, and how Akhenaten is the born son of the solar orb and so forth and so on. On the surface they appear to embrace the idea that this is an egalitarian and cosmopolitan religion, a religion that is for everybody. Akhenaten's only work that we know of is the 'The Hymn to the Aten'. Even though many people gush over its beauty, I personally find that the verses have all of the depth and spirituality of a bag of stale potato chips. But at this point I freely confess that in my opinion the highest points of Egyptian funerary literature were the Pyramid Texts that were written thousands of years before Akhenaten was born.

The artwork, on the other hand, tells a different story. Why? Well as we explore the tombs of the nobles and other dignitaries, Egyptologists noticed that the Aten's outstretched arms with their life-giving Ankh hands only touch Akhenaten and his family; strangely for some reason they always fall short of non-royalty, and of course the commoners, as usual, are nowhere to be seen. Before long it slowly becomes obvious that this wasn't a religion for everybody, no in fact it actually has more of the trappings of an imperial cult; one that is designed exclusively for the royal family and no one else.

But what was life like at Akhet-Aten itself? Well, in other surviving murals we see Akhenaten playing with his daughters as he and Nefertiti share food with each other. In the temples there are offering tables heaped high with food for the sun god. And finally in a touching scene we see a reluctant Akhenaten snapping the neck of a goose or duck in sacrifice to the Aten. Clearly, he is a sensitive man who is attuned to the needs of all.

His artwork is usually praised as being realistic and that he was devoted to 'ma'at' which means 'truth' in Ancient Egyptian.

But what about the commoners? You know the proverbial person in the street? What were their lives like?

Clearly from the murals they too must have had a wonderful life. To start with, there obviously was an abundance of food. After all, if they could pile it high on top of dozens of offering tables in the great temple of the Aten then there was plenty to go around. It was obvious that everybody was fell fed and happy and from there we can infer that this extended to the common folk as well.

The reality is completely different. In fact, life for the poor looked more like Franz Kafka's "In the Penal Colony" meets the ninth circle of Dante's "Inferno".

We know for a fact that it was a living hell instead of heaven on earth. Why do I say this? Well because one of the enigmas of Amarna studies is the fact that even though we know thousands of people lived in Akhet-Aten archeologists had never found a single grave of an ordinary person who had lived there. This was a complete mystery. For over a hundred years the only exceptions to this 'no burial rule' were Akhenaten's royal tomb, which had been desecrated, along with a handful of tombs for the nobility many of which were unfinished and show no sign of being used. However, there were no graves of the ordinary people. Somebody somewhere had to die, and when that happened, they had to be buried.

So, where did all these bodies go?

Speculations abounded; maybe they were thrown in the river. Perhaps they were the victims of a putative plague and their bodies burned. Or maybe they were transported back to Thebes and buried there. The question remained unanswered for over a century. And then recently the problem was solved once and for all, when excavations discovered the graves of thousands of people, all buried well outside of the city of Akhet-Aten.

Now the dark side of Akhet-Aten was discovered. To start with none of these people had been mummified. But then things grew even darker; after forensic anthropologists looked at the skeletons it turned out that they had all died in their late teens or early twenties. And then it became even more sinister; even though we know there was an abundant supply of food at Akeht-Aten, all of the skeletons showed that they had suffered from severe malnutrition, arthritis, and broken bones all as a result of the slave work, they were forced to perform. Undoubtedly, they labored from the day they arrived in Akhet-Aten until the day they died. After their deaths their broken and discarded bodies were tossed into a hole in the middle of the desert far from the glorious city of Akhet-Aten. Alas these poor people were buried with virtually nothing except the clothes they were wearing. There were no grave goods of any kind interred with them. There were no shawbti's, the miniature statues that would perform work for them in the next world, no heart scarabs to ensure their passage to the next world, no scraps from The Book of the Dead, and with the exception of two burials, none were interred in a coffin. This stood in stark contrast to the fabulous tombs of the nobles where the dead were buried with everything that they would need for the next life. In contrast these poor unmarked graves, empty of any grave goods, speak volumes about these people's short brutal lives.

The conclusion is fairly obvious; For the rich and famous, while they were living, life was a fun filled cabaret. Blindfolded musicians played at every meal, and from time to time the king and queen would toss gold necklaces from their balcony to the obsequious noblemen groveling beneath them. And once the grand party came to an end and they died, they were granted a lavish tomb in which to reside for eternity. However, the ordinary person's life to quote Thomas Hobbes was 'solitary, poor, brutish, and short.'

The important part of history is to try to gather all of the evidence together in one place, and then objectively interpret it. When we do this a different picture emerges. Instead of the usual portrait of Akhenaten as a starry-eyed philosopher king whose sole thoughts were on his people, and his religion. In this new more comprehensive view, he looks more like a self-absorbed monomaniac, who created a rather superficial, ethical free, solar cult devoid of any underlying philosophy. The 'Atenist revolution' when it's stripped of its trappings is little more than an exclusive royal cult that extends only as far as the sycophantic nobility and that's it. His new religion offers nothing for the common people in this life except to be worked to death, and nothing in the life to follow once you die. The only thing that is clear is that Akhenaten is the sole prophet of his religion and his immediate family and courtiers are the exclusive recipients of the Aten's gifts. When one considers all of these facts it's hardly surprising the cult barely survived the death of its founder and the violent demolition that took place after its demise. In the end it's clear that the idea that Akhet-Aten was some kind of Xanadu and the ideal that this an egalitarian society is fatally flawed.

Interestingly, even though Akhenaten was busy turning Egypt upside down theologically with his new religion, there is surprisingly no mention of it anywhere in the letters. This strengthens the conjecture that Atenism was a local religion and that Akhenaten had no intention of spreading the gospel of his new monotheism beyond the borders of Egypt.

Chapter 8

Fear and Loathing in the Northern Levant

Introducing the Apiru

Now having given a thumb-nail sketch of life in Egypt we'll shift our focus to the Levant and Northern Lebanon in order to see what is going on there.

The first time I read the Amarna letters I kept noticing the mention of a shadowy, enigmatic, and sinister group of people lurking in the background who were known simply as the 'Apiru' (alternate spelling "Hapiru").   I wondered who they were. It was clear from the letters that they weren't part of any nation state like the Hittites, Mitannians or the Egyptians. So, since they clearly play a major role in our story it only makes sense to slow down and spend a chapter investigating just who these infuriatingly enigmatic, and elusive people were before we continue in our narrative.

In order to unravel this historical Gordian knot, I checked the index to find out how often they were mentioned. I quickly discovered that the 'Apiru' were the second most frequently mentioned group, the Egyptians being first.   So based on that slim observation you would think that we would know quite a lot about them. The truth is we don't.

The problem is that there are no records of who they are, where they came from, or what happened to them.   It's impossible to determine who they are from the internal references in the letters, since all the references to them were always dismissive and derogatory; never flattering. For instance, if a group of people defected from one mayor to another then they had become 'one with the Apiru'. Another problem is that it's obvious that both the author and the recipient of the letters knew exactly who the 'Apiru' were and therefore no explanation of who they were was needed.

The problem is that the word 'Apiru' itself doesn't have a specific meaning. As far as we can tell it doesn't refer to any geographic reference or historical personage. Linguists had noted a similarity between the name 'Apiru' and 'Hebrew' and at first it was conjectured that the Apiru were the early Hebrews. This has since been discarded for numerous reasons and as a result I was right back at square one; who were the Apiru?

So far it appears that they were desert nomads who would hire themselves out as mercenaries. However, we should never lose sight of the fact that even this is conjectural. The one thing that emerges from the letters is that Abdi-Asirta, one of the villains of our story, regularly formed alliances with this shadowy group to attack Rib-Hadda and his cities. And it is obvious that Rib-Hadda and the various other writers of the Amarna letters are afraid of them.

I was fascinated, by what I had discovered and continued reading these disjointed and unconnected references to them and unsurprisingly, I continued to be baffled by what I found. To start with I kept wondering how could such a group of people who were playing such a major role on the stage in the Northern Levant have escaped the historical record?

The Apiru were like a desert mirage, they appeared suddenly and then vanished just as quickly. However, piecing the fragmentary information together we can form a picture of them; they were apparently a stateless, amorphous group of marauders who hired themselves out as mercenaries. Their main order of business seemed to be that they were hired killers who would assassinate mayors, rob caravans, align themselves with various mayors, or act as *agent provocateurs* stirring up the population to revolt against their lords. The one thing that is clear is that the Apiru were an anonymous and deadly force to deal with.

In that case then the next question was, were there any other references to them in the source material from Egypt and the Hittites?

I dug deeper and read as much of the fragmentary material that was preserved from the capital of Amarna that I could find. And unsurprisingly there was no mention of the Apiru at all at Akhet-Aten. As usual the only thing that was going on there was the perpetual motion party machine and the daily salute to how wonderful Akhenaten, and Nefertiti were.

Next, I turned to the Hittite documents and discovered there was no mention of the Apiru in any of them.

It appeared to be a complete dead end.

Alright so how do we solve the problem of discovering who the Apiru were? Well, since I'm an advanced microscopist, with some training in biotechnology, along with being a big fan of crime shows and detective series, I've discovered the awesome power of assembling all of the evidence first and then scrubbing it vigorously and usually before long the truth emerges. In this case what I did was collate every mention of the word 'Apiru' in the Amarna letters in order to get a sense of who they were and what their relationships were to the various people in the narrative.

A close reading of the Amarna letters shows that the Apiru were more sophisticated than they appear. To start with they definitely had some kind of an espionage system in place. They were literate since they had scribes who could write to the various mayors of the cities and threaten them. As such this implies, that no matter how simple it was, a communication network of some kind was in place.

Additionally, it appears they had very organized military forces that would ally themselves with the various partisans in the levant at the time. And then at the granular level they had trained assassins who could infiltrate the various palaces and carry out successful murders of targeted individuals. Not only that but the Apiru had *agent provocateurs* who could ingratiate themselves within the general population in order to undermine the cities morale. Drawing all of these clues together the tentative conclusion is that even though the Apiru were a 'stateless' people, they were still one of the power brokers in local politics in the Northern Levant and a force to be reckoned with. What emerges is a more complex picture of the 'Apiru' than had been suspected before. However, the fact that they disappear abruptly from the historical record after the Amarna period closes, suggests they were ultimately absorbed into the general population and forgotten about.

We'll continue to explore the machinations of the Apiru in the Levant as our story evolves.

Chapter 9

Ammuru, Gubla, Sumur, Beirut, and Rib-Hadda

As we move deeper and deeper into our story, we find that it revolves primarily around several locations; Ammuru, Gubla, Sumur, Byblos, and Beirut.

The first one is Ammuru. In his letters Rib-Hadda rails constantly against the fall of Ammuru. Clearly the location and importance of Ammuru were well known to Rib-Hadda and everybody connected with the Amarna correspondence since he never defines what it is or where it is. The only problem is that in the 3500 years that have passed 'Ammuru' has vanished, undoubtedly absorbed into dozens of different empires that had risen and fallen since then.

From what I can see "Ammuru" doesn't appear to be a distinct geographic location like Washington D.C., London, Moscow, or Beijing. Instead, it appears to be a vague all-purpose geographical term like the "Mid-east" or "Central Africa or "South America" that gives you a general idea of what you're talking about. However, I hasten to add that all of this is conjecture based on the fact that I can't find any general definition of what or where Ammuru was or its significance is in the bronze age in the scholastic literature.

The next city is Gubla. Gubla is located in Lebanon and one of the oldest continually occupied cities in the world.

Sumur is currently located in Syria and was one of the main cities that was in Rib-Hadda's domain.

Beirut, is of course, the present-day capital of Lebanon and was the final point of exile for Rib-Hadda where he was eventually assassinated.

Chapter: 10

The Echoes of Other Voices from the Past

As I continued to wander through the Amarna Hall of Mirrors, I began noticing venomous references that Rib-Hadda made about various other people. At first, I was alarmed by all of these *ad hominems* and wondered if they were true. And then after a while, you begin to get used to them until you finally start to ignore them because they're usually just vague assertions about 'treacherous deeds' being performed by one person which are then followed up by the strident and hysterical denials of the other person, who then accuses the first person of being a liar.

The problem is what the details of the treacherous deeds are is almost never spelled out and as such you're left scratching your head wondering what is going on? However, in this never-ending desert soap opera I noticed a few names that kept recurring so frequently that I began to suspect that there might, in fact, be some truth to the accusations. The men mentioned most frequently were Abdi-Asirta, Aziru (Abdi Asirta's' son), Zimredda, and Yanhamu we will meet them at various points in the Amarna letters.

Abdi-Asirta

Every story needs a villain; you know the person who stands in opposition to everything the hero is trying to accomplish. And unsurprisingly that rule holds firm in our tale of the life and times of Rib-Hadda.

As we've already mentioned not only was Rib-Hadda caught between the three superpowers of the middle east, the Hittites, the Mitannians, and the Egyptians, he also had problems to deal with in his own backyard; problems that would ultimately destroy him.

Alright, so who is the villain in this tale? Well, the main one (and the deadliest) goes by the name of Abdi-Asirta (Also spelled Abdi Astarti).

Abdi-Asirta is to Rib-Hadda what Moriarty is to Sherlock Holmes, what the Joker is to Batman or Darth Vader is to Obi Wan Kenobe. To hear Rib-Hadda tell it the man is a perennial menace, a mastermind of duplicity and treachery with zero redeeming qualities to him, a man he constantly refers to as a 'treacherous dog'.

What was Abdi-Asirta like? Well, once again all we know of Abdi- Asirta is contained in a single letter that he wrote to a commissioner, along with Rib-Hadda's venomous diatribes against him.

The one thing that is clear from Rib-Hadda's letters, and subsequent history is that Abdi-Asirta had two paramount goals in mind. In no particular order they were 1) kill Rib-Hadda, and 2) take over his cities. Once that happened then would break away from the Egyptian empire and rule over his own micro-kingdom. And in order to achieve these goals Abdi-Asirta he used the aforementioned "Apiru" to achieve his goal.

So, in the immortal words of Pontius Pilate "What is the truth?" Who was Abdi-Asirta? Was he really 'the treacherous dog' that Rib-Hadda describes him as, or was there another aspect to the man that we don't know about?

We'll explore all of these possibilities in awhile

E.A. 62 Abdi-Asirta read the letter from his commissioner Panhanate. Once again one of the treacherous dogs that roamed the Northern Levant had taken it upon themselves, to report his raid on Sumur to the commissioner. And now the commissioner had written him a blistering letter demanding an explanation as to what had happened.

That was the bad news.

The good news was that the commissioner could rarely be stirred from his residence to personally investigate what was going on in the provinces, after all more than one commissioner had wound up dead after investigating things too closely and sticking his unwanted nose in the wrong snake hole. The problem was that accidents happened all the time in the desert, and death was the constant companion of every man who lived there and murders were never investigated.

Instead, Abdi-Asirta would send him a tablet filled with honey coated lies that would lull the commissioner back to sleep and then after the usual exchange of tablets it would die down and be forgotten about. After that Abdi-Asirta would go back to his plan to overthrow Rib-Hadda take his cities and then eventually form his own kingdom and to rule among the leaders of the world.

But that was still in the future.

The scribe picked up his stylus and began writing on the soft clay and Abdi-Asirta began dictating his letter to the commissioner.

"Say to my Lord the commissioner…" Abdi-Asirta began.

EA 62 Is a fascinating letter. In this letter Abdi-Asirta is writing directly to his commissioner Pahanate and not the king. The fact that it wound up in Akhet-Aten proves that, for unknown reasons, it must have been forwarded by Panhanate to the palace. Apparently, the eyes of the king were everywhere.

However, in this letter Abdi-Asirta disposed of the usual formulaic debasements that are the hallmark of letters to the king. Instead, Abdi-Asirta simply says that he throws himself at the feet of the commissioner, before launching into a defensive attack in answer to the questions that the commissioner had evidently asked him. Apparently, the commissioner had received messages that Abdi-Asirta was busy undermining Rib-Hadda (who isn't mentioned by name.).

According to this unnamed accuser Abdi-Asirta had attacked him with his forces. The one thing that is clear so far, is that the anonymous correspondent who had written the letter to the commissioner, had obviously survived the attack and was able to write a scathing report to the commissioner about Abdi-Asirta's activities describing him as a 'treacherous dog'.

Apparently, this lost letter to the commissioner triggered a reply from the same commissioner, who then wrote an even more scalding letter to Abdi-Asirta accusing him of being a traitor to the king and Egypt. Serious charges that could have profound results on Abdi-Asirta if they were true.

Unsurprisingly Abdi-Asirta's version of the raid is completely different from the one that the commissioner received. In Abdi-Asirta's new improved version of this tempest in a teapot, he is the portrait of hurt innocence, and boundless courage, all blended with unflagging loyalty to the Pharaoh. No, what really happened, according to Abdi-Asirta, was while he was resting comfortably at his home in Irqata, when it came to his attention that the city of Sumur was under attack. So, rather than continue with this leisurely lifestyle he instantly sprang into action, and galloped off to Sumur.

Then as he approached the city, he discovered to his dismay there were no troops defending it in the attack from Sehlal. After he arrived at the palace, he found, much to his chagrin, that it had been abandoned and was now only guarded by four men. They, of course, begged him to save them from the troops of Sehlal and like the loyal servant to the king that he was, he granted them their wish.

But Abdi-Asirta doesn't stop there. He carefully pivots and turns from defense to offense. Evidently, he received information that the other mayors had also been writing to the Pharaoh complaining about Abdi-Asirta infringing on their territories; an accusation that he denies emphatically calling them in no uncertain terms 'liars' in the closing lines of his letter.

What happens next? Alas, we're plunged back into the eternal darkness of another Amarna night because at that point the letter closes.

Unfortunately, all we know of Abdi-Asirta comes from two sources; one is a letter that he wrote that has survived the ravages of time. And of course, the only other is Rib-Hadda's scathing diatribes against him.

Abdi-Asirta makes his sole appearance in EA 59 in a letter he wrote to an unnamed commissioner.

The opening of his letter contains the usual sycophantic blather however the obsequies contain one thing that is notable; they are shorter than Rib-Hadda's salutations. Mercifully, he gets to the point much faster than his loquacious colleague.

Turning to the contents of the letter itself we discover that Abdi-Asirta answers to a commissioner named 'Panhanete'. While Rib-Hadda on the other hand answers to a different commissioner a man named 'Panhamata'. There are a few things which can be divined from this fragment. To start with since both men answer to someone further up the ladder than they are, it is clear that there is some sort of bureaucratic hierarchy in place in the Levant. Expanding on this slim clue we can assume that Rib-Hadda and Abdi-Asirta probably held equivalent positions in the Egyptian administration.

However, everything also seems to point to the fact that they both were at the bottom of the royal pyramid. In today's management style they might be called 'front line managers.

Turning to the main part of the letter Abdi-Asirta asserts that he is guarding the cities of Sumur and Ullasa. This is interesting because Sumur, as we'll soon discover, is the same city that Rib-Hadda is apparently in charge of. This makes me wonder if they had overlapping or different responsibilities for the same cities. Or more likely was Abdi-Asirta trying to usurp Rib-Hadda's control of Sumur, by asserting that he's the one who is defending the city?

Perhaps the telling point is that Abdi-Asirta makes the rather interesting side comment that he guards the grain of Sumur. The implication from this comment is that Sumur has plenty of food and there's nothing to worry about. However, when we turn to Rib-Hadda's letters he states that he is running out of supplies. This leads to an interesting question; did Abdi-Asirta control the food supply and was he trying to starve Rib-Hadda into submission? And if he did does it explain Rib-Hadda's never ending complaint that he is running out of supplies? Or is this just another dead end in the Amarna letters? Unsurprisingly, there's no unequivocal answer in the letters.

Ammunira

EA 141   Once again after we plow our way through the usual blandishments about how wonderful the king is, we get to the heart of the letter. The king is clearly fed up with everything that is going on in Ammuru and is sending in troops to secure the area. Ammunira swears undying loyalty and agrees to place his troops and everything that he has at the king's disposal.

EA 142   In this letter Ammunira simply says that he will prepare the city for the arrival of the king's archers. And then he assures the king that the ruler of Gubla is residing with him, and he notes that the man has given the sons of Rib-Hadda, who is also there with him to the rebels who are in Ammuru.

EA 143   This letter is so fragmented that it's impossible to determine what is going on in it.

Zimreddi

All we know of Zimreddi is contained in two letters along with scattered references to him throughout the rest of the letters.

As usual like virtually every single correspondent before and after him he tells us how he rejoiced at receiving the king's letter. In fact, to hear Zimreddi tell it his eyes lit up like the winning slot machine in a Las Vegas casino. And his heart was fluttering away like a million butterflies in spring as he read every word that the pharaoh had to say to him with ecstatic, almost orgasmic joy. And once again he swears absolute undivided and unswerving loyalty to the monarch, with all of the usual promises to obey every single word that the pharaoh tells him. Finally, he assures the king that he has made preparations for the arrival of the King's archers that will retake the cities that have allied themselves with the Apiru.

EA 145   In this second very fragmented letter Zimreddi says that the war against him is very severe and that he is losing control of the hinterlands. This is cloaked in the euphemism of 'The King's breath does not reach the hinterlands.

Aziru

After his father is murdered Aziru takes over as head of the clan that is trying to dispose of Rib-Hadda. Aziru continues in his never-ending attempt to get rid of Rib-Hadda once and for all.

In this subset of letters, we finally get a view of the inner workings of Aziru's micro-empire as he tries to expand his domain, while simultaneously avoiding the wrath of the pharaoh and deftly maneuvering around his fellow mayors who are also at war with him.

There are at least sixteen letters in the Aziru corpus either from Aziru or addressed to Aziru. Even though this subset of letters is small we at least get a glimpse into the inner thoughts of the mastermind that took over after Abdi-Asirta died.

Another thing that is puzzling it that while Rib-Hadda is ranting and raving about how Abdi-Asirta (and after Abdi-Asirta's death his son Aziru's) is constantly at war with both him and the other cities in the Levan. However, in Aziru's letters there isn't any mention of Rib-

Hadda. Actually, the bulk of Aziru's letters deal with his never-ending attempts to get out of visiting the Pharaoh in Egypt for reasons that he never specifies.

Another fact emerges from his letters is the fact that Aziru is a nuanced Machiavellian who can shrewdly blend the truth with lies while deftly playing the game of international politics while carefully avoiding the assassin's knife that felled both his father and Rib-Hadda.

EA 156 *Aziru read the king's letter. Once again, the king demanded that Aziru appear before him in the royal court at Akhet-Aten. But currently Aziru didn't dare leave for Egypt; things were delicately balanced between the various mayors with each one watching and waiting to attack the others. If Aziru were to leave for Egypt now it would be seen as a sign of weakness and the surrounding mayors would attack him and things would spin out of control. So instead of leaving the Levant he would send his two sons to the Pharaoh.*

This letter undoubtedly is an answer to a letter where the king demands that Aziru return to Egypt for unspecified reasons. In this brief and frustrating message from Aziru we see that he has clearly been avoiding seeing the pharaoh. Unfortunately, for us Aziru never tells us the real reason that he refuses to return to Egypt.

Aziru opens by making the usual claims to be absolutely loyal, the king's obedient servant, that he is nothing but the dirt beneath his feet. And then since Aziru who is the king of the weasels, deflects about returning to Egypt and instead says that he is sending his two sons, to be the king's 'servants' (i.e., hostages) and that they are to do as the king orders. In return Aziru simply asks that he be left in Ammuru.

But as we will discover in the ensuing letters that Aziru is a master of avoiding the pharaoh, and pretty much anybody else who gets in his way.

EA 157 *Aziru read the letter from the king over and over again. "Say to Aziru the King your lord... and know that I am hale and hearty like the sun and everything goes very well for me." Aziru mulled over the letter. As usual, the King wanted Aziru to report personally to Egypt. And even though he had sent his two sons as 'servants to the king, it apparently wasn't enough to placate his majesty.*

The one theme that constantly floats through Aziru's letters is the fact that the king wants him to return to Egypt and unsurprisingly Aziru has a never-ending series of excuses for staying in Ammurru.

This letter appears to be the response to a different letter, now lost, where the King as usual demands that Aziru return to Egypt for reasons that are never spelled out. Aziru on the other hand in his sycophantic way simultaneously professes his unswerving loyalty to the king and willingness to see him. This time the only thing that stands between him and returning to Egypt so that he can view the face of his majesty in all of his glory, is the fact that the magnates of Sumur are stopping him from leaving the city.

But that's just one problem Aziru has to deal with. Not only that but he has apparently been accused of dereliction of duties (by whom we never find out). A charge that, he firmly denies.

After that Aziru pivots and now deftly plays the Hittite card, not only are the magnates forbidding from leaving Ammuru, there's an even bigger problem looming on the horizon. The ubiquitous Hittites are preparing for war against him. In closing Aziru asks for troops and chariots to help him. A request that is apparently denied.

EA 158   This letter is different from the others. In this one Aziru is writing to his 'father' Tutu. Since we know that Tutu isn't Aziru's biological father (that was of course Abdi-Asirta), it is clear that this is an honorific title meant to show respect to somebody who is your superior.

Aziru opens the letter in his usual gushing manner swearing that whatever he has in his possession is also Tutu's and therefore it also belongs to the king. All he has to do is write asking for whatever he wants, and Aziru will send it to him. This predictable, and monotonous, formulaic debasement runs through the Amarna letters like dirty water running through a street gutter before vanishing down a storm drain. Frankly, after a while you wish that the recipient would call the other person's bluff and say "Okay send me everything you own, I need it right now." and after that see what happens. But alas they never do.

Unsurprisingly, Aziru says that treacherous men are slandering him and then in typical Amarna letters style never spells out what these slanders are. In closing he reaffirms his loyalty to the king.

EA 159 AZIRU This is a letter responding to a letter sent from the pharaoh demanding that Aziru rebuild the city of Sumur. One of the irritating problems with this letter is that both the King and Aziru are obviously thoroughly familiar with whatever happened to Sumur, the problem is that we don't have a clue as to what happened in Sumur. It's fairly obvious from the repeated assurances is that Aziru makes is that he is going to rebuild Sumur just as soon as he can get around to it. Hopefully that will be no more than a year or two. Maybe three to four but no more than five years at the most. The one thing that is clear is that from Aziru's constant reassurances that he is going to be rebuild Sumur, it's that the king's original letter must have bordered on incendiary that Sumur be rebuilt.

And finally in closing Aziru, blasts all the mayors saying they are traitors to him and lying about him without ever specifying what these lies are.

EA 160   As usual Aziru seems to be remiss in pleasing the king. This time it appears that the king is upset about an unfulfilled demand for 'boxwood' that the king had clearly ordered. And it's obvious that it wasn't delivered. This naturally led to a "where-the-hell-is-my-order-of-boxwood' tablet from the king.

Predictably Aziru opens his letter by reaffirming his loyalty to the king. And then in response to the missing boxwood order, Aziru claims that he is preparing eight ships loaded with boxwood and logs right now as he is writing.   And since there is no further mention of 'boxwood' in any of the subsequent letters it's safe to say that they probably arrived in Egypt.

The king also wants to know why Aziru hasn't rebuilt Sumur. Evidently the other 'treacherous mayors', that Aziru is always screaming about are doing everything they can to undermine Aziru. Apparently, these other mayors are letting the Pharaoh know that zero progress has been made on this urban renewal project. Aziru replies saying that the kings of Nuhasse have been at war with him and that, unsurprisingly, this has slowed down progress. However, there's nothing to worry about; Aziru promises to rebuild Sumur this year.

He closes by asking the king to send Aziru's messenger back (apparently the messenger was 'detained' for some reason) along with the king's own messenger so they can bring the tribute back to the king.

EA 161   In this letter Aziru appears to play the part of Charles Dickens famous pickpocket Jack Dawkins AKA "The Artful Dodger" in Dickens' novel Oliver Twist.

Dickens describes Jack Dawkins as *"... of a rather saturnine disposition, and seldom gave way to merriment when it interfered with business, rifled Oliver's pockets with steady assiduity."* In this case instead of 'Jack Dawkins' it was his possible ancient predecessor, Aziru who was industriously rifling the king's pocket with steady assiduity as he promised the king everything while delivering just enough to hold the king's wrath at bay.

Again, this letter is clearly a response to another lost letter that the king wrote to Aziru with a number of grievances in it. First and foremost, the king is asking him why he didn't greet his messenger Hani. From other letters we know that Hani was clearly one of the major players in the King's cabinet and to snub him was a major diplomatic *faux pax*. We also know from previous letters that the king always sends letters in advance telling his vassals to prepare for the arrival of his representatives so that they can make sure that they have everything they need. This is always followed by a confirmation letter from the vassal back to the king, assuring the king that he has received the monarch's letter and not to worry, everything will be provided in abundance for the king's representative.

But in this case Aziru apparently missed the clay mail because he is nowhere to be seen when Hani shows up. The suspicious pharaoh then accuses Aziru of hiding in Tunip, a charge that Aziru unsurprisingly, and stridently denies.

Now, for one of the few times in the Letters we get a glimpse into the 'slanders' that are supposedly being spread about Aziru. Apparently, somebody told the king about this blunder and the king in turn decides to put Aziru on the spot. Aziru slips out of this one like an eel escaping an open net, by telling the king to ignore the treacherous men who are speaking lies about him. In this case he innocently claims that he was actually residing in Tunip, and had no idea that Hani had arrived. However, once he heard that Hani had arrived, he tried to catch up with him, but surprise, surprise! As usual Azuru is a day late and a dollar short, and doesn't make it in time to see Hani. The man has left Ammurru. But, just to show there's no ill will Aziru assures the king that Hani was well taken care of by his brothers and Bet-ili. They gave him oxen, and horses, and birds for food along with strong drink. Aziru then says that he gave Hani horses and asses for his journey home. Aziru then quickly pivots and says that once he appears in Egypt that Hani will defend him.

Aziru continues to tap dance faster and faster saying that the reason the building in Sumur has stopped is because of the fact that the Kings of Nuhasse are at war with him. As we've already seen Aziru, like a mediocre poker player, who has already played this card before. This time he spins the tale a little bit saying things have gotten worse in Ammuru. It turns out that not only is he at war with Nuhasse there was also an insurrection led by Hatip.

Aziru doesn't stop there. Not at all, in fact he's just getting started as he tries to bury Hatip a little deeper in the warm desert sand by accusing him of taking half of everything that the king had given to Aziru. In fact, to hear Aziru tell it, all of the gold and silver that the king gave to Aziru has now been taken by Hatip! In fact, if we're to believe Aziru (and who would doubt the integrity of a fine upstanding and loyal subject of the king like him) he is flat broke.

After that we see the first evidence of Aziru's contacts with the Hittites. How do we know this? Will in the closing sentences the king complains that when a messenger from Hatti arrived in Ammuru, the man had been given everything that he wanted. However, when the Pharaoh sent his man to Aziru he received nothing! This is rather interesting contradiction because Aziru has repeatedly used the Hittites an excuse not to return to Egypt. And now (will wonders never cease?) whatever problems he had with the Hittites have now vanished. The king is of course wondering why Aziru is inexplicably courting the Hittites. Aziru, like a good tennis ball player knocks the ball into a different part of the court and deflects telling the king to send him his messenger so that he can give him everything he desires, food, supplies, ships, logs of boxwood and other kinds of wood.

EA 162   This is probably the most remarkable letter in the whole Amarna corpus. This is one of the rare letters that we have from the Pharaoh addressed to a vassal where he doesn't just hand out orders for women, silver and glass. No, in this letter we get a direct insight into the Pharaoh's thought processes as he analyzes both the pros and cons of the contradictory information that he's obviously received from various sources and then tries to piece together what is the truth and after that formulate a winning strategy.

To begin with he refers to the ruler of Byblos whose brother cast him away at the gate, this is a clear reference to Rib-Hadda and it's obvious that he knows that Aziru knows he is referring to the time when Rib-Hadda's own brother prevented him from entering the city.

The fact that the Pharaoh always refers to Rib-Hadda in the third person is telling in itself. But amazingly he says that Rib-Hadda tried to make a deal with Aziru in a plot against Rib-Hadda's own brother. Evidently, he told Aziru that there was gold in the city, and that he would give it to Aziru if Aziru overthrew Rib-Hadda's brother. At the time Rib-Hadda was residing in Sidon and then for reasons that are obscure Aziru instead betrays Rib-Hadda by handing him over to some other mayors.

If this sounds confusing it is, but this is just another twist in the never-ending mystery of the Amarna Hall of Mirrors.

The pharaoh then goes on to complain about other things that Aziru has done. Evidently Aziru has formed an alliance with the king of Qidsa since he has taken food and strong drink with him. The king then wonders why Aziru is switching sides. And then he presciently warns Aziru that the people that he is befriending are actually preparing a fire, and that when the time is right, they will throw him into it.

Which as we know from subsequent history is exactly what happens.

After that the king issues one of the most blood curdling threats in the Amarna letters, he tells Aziru that if he is plotting treachery against the king, then the King will execute him and his entire family by the 'axe of the king'. The King follows it up with a not so veiled threat that if the King chooses to invade the area he will win.

Finally, the king addresses Aziru's refusal to come to Egypt. The King clearly knows Aziru has weaseled his way out of it once before, and now the king demands that either Aziru comes to Egypt or have his son delivered instead.

Next the king grants Aziru's request that Hanni the king's emissary be sent to receive prisoners that will be sent to Egypt where they will undoubtedly, be executed. Copper fetters are supposed to be put on their legs, among the people are Sarru along with all of his sons, Leya along with all of his sons, the son in law of Manya along with his sons and their wives.

Unfortunately, we don't know what happened to all of these people.

EA 164 AZIRU This is a letter from Aziru probably to a commissioner named Tutu. He says that Hattip is staying with him and they will eventually, one of these days, make the journey to Egypt. Aziru sends his regrets that he can't return to the palace because the Hittites are at Nuhasse and he would be remiss in his duties if he left Ammur at this time. No, instead, Aziru argues that it's better for him to wait until after the Hittites leave.

After that Aziru then makes a rather bizarre digression and says (perhaps after receiving the previous letter where the king threatens to execute Aziru and his family.) that he is afraid both of the king and Tutu, and therefore wants to them swear an oath that they will do nothing treacherous against Aziru. Which is sort of like the fox asking the farmer not to kill him if he raids the chicken coop one more time.

EA 165 AZIRU In this letter Aziru reiterates that he and Hatip would willingly come to Egypt, except for the fact that now Tunip is threatened and the Hittites are still in Nuhasse and as such he is worried that if he leaves, the Hittites will come to Amurru. Aziru assures the king that the moment the Hittites leave Nuhasse that he and Hatip will be on their way to the palace. In the meantime, Aziru points out that it is only a two-day march for the Hittites from Tunip from Nuhasse. Of course, he doesn't say what he's going do to stop the Hittites, if they decide to invade Ammurru, because as we discover in a later letter that there's a minimum of 90,000 Hittite troops in the area.

Aziru, in his role as the conductor of 'The One Note Symphony' closes with the usual monotonous plea not to listen to treacherous men, and to ignore him as he plots his own treacherous acts against the various mayors.

He finally closes by saying he, his brothers and his sons are loyal servants of the king.

EA 166 AZIRU This epistle from Aziru is written to a man named Haay whom he refers to as his 'brother'. From the context of the letter, it's obvious that Haay isn't Aziru's biological brother; after all we know that Aziru's brothers are actively working to kill Rib-Hadda and taking over his territories. In this case, Haay was clearly an equal in the hierarchy and therefore he referred to him as 'his brother' instead of 'his father' which Aziru would have used if he was writing to a superior.

In this case Haay obviously had received a letter from the king ordering him to light a fire under Aziru's butt in order to get him to return to Egypt and visit his majesty the king. However, Aziru in his usual florid manner assures Haay that he is in fact the loyal, undying servant of the king, who unhesitatingly looks forward to seeing the gracious face of the king, and then reassures Haay that in addition to that all of Aziru' sons and brothers are also servants of the king. Next, he says that he and Hatip are in fact leaving for Egypt just as soon as he finishes writing this letter. And then right on schedule Aziru, like a prima donna ballerina in the Bolshoi ballet, spins like a top, leaps into the air and lands on the well-worn dime of his one-size- fits-all-excuse that he can't leave for the palace because the Hittites are still in Nuhasse and as a result he can't leave Amurru. So it is with the greatest reluctance that he continues to stay in place until the Hittites depart. However, he assures Haay that once the Hittites leave, he and Hatip will depart for Egypt as soon as practical.

EA 167 AZIRU In this letter the King, once again, has clearly demanded that Aziru return to Egypt, and once again, with same monotonous predictability Aziru plays the same old Hittite card only this time he claims that the Hittite King is in Nuhasse. Clearly Suppiluliumas is either planning to invade Mitannia, or has invaded Mitannia and this lends significant credibility to Aziru's concerns about the Hittite threat. And just to emphasize how threatening this is he claims that they are in Nuhasse and only two days march from Tunip. He reassures Tutu that he will arrive in Egypt, eventually, and hopes that Tutu is safe and sound and that he will see the king as possible.

EA 168 AZIRU Finally in this incredibly short and fragmentary letter evidently Aziru has either run out of excuses or the Hittites have finally departed and it is clear that Aziru is finally sailing for Egypt.

EA 169 *Aziru's son read the letter from one of the mayors. It was a reference to a letter from the King of Nuhasse that had written to the pharaoh, accusing him of selling his father Aziru to the king of Egypt in exchange for gold. The fact that Aziru had willingly gone to Egypt after the Hittites had left the area that they were occupying had been conveniently ignored.*

This letter was probably written by Aziru's son DU-Tessup given these facts it was time to ask the king to release Aziru so that he could return home safe and sound. Because of that Aziru is now trapped in Egypt with no way of getting out! He asks that Aziru be released immediately from Egypt. And then it closes with what looks like a not-so-subtle threat to go to war if these demands aren't met.

EA 170 AZIRU Aziru's *sons had deployed his spies along the northern border of Ammuru to monitor the Hittites, now that spring was here and the grass was growing there would be fodder for the horses and food for the army. For the first few weeks they saw nothing, and then they caught sight of the first trickle of the river that formed the Hittite army. Initially it was just a half-dozen scouts, forward observers or so that were surveying the land, looking for Mitannian or Egyptian patrols that might be guarding the frontier a few random spies were to be expected.*

And then behind them came the giant army itself. First the light armor, then the chariots, armorers, heavy infantry. After that there were the 'camp followers' or what might be called the 'two-legged black market' that consisted of a much smaller army of prostitutes, merchants, and various people who supplied the comforts of life that the Hittite military couldn't provide as efficiently or cheaply as they could.

The spies watched from a safe distance for days as the huge river of men flowed passed them and they calculated that there were about 90,000 troops on the march to somewhere but fortunately it wasn't Ammuru.

And then like good spies they faded into the background and their reports made it back to headquarters and from there to Baalyua, Aziru's son, who then relayed the information to his father Aziru who was stuck in Egypt trying to get back to Ammuru.

This is another letter from another one of Aziru's sons named Baaluya sent to his father Aziru who was being 'detained' in Egypt. Apparently, there are ongoing negotiations to get Aziru out of Egypt as soon as possible. But what they consist of is never disclosed.

Now, the Hittites are on the move under the leadership of a Hittite general named Lupakku; evidently, he has already taken Amqu and then allied himself with other cities and have taken Aadumi. Baaluya. He claims that the Hittite general Zitana has come and there are 90,000 infantrymen with him. But Baaluya reassures him that these are unconfirmed rumors and that he is sending other spies to verify it.

EA 171 In this epistle near the middle of the letter we get an accusation that Aziru has sent messengers to the king but for some reason Yanhamu is forbidding him from sending them to Egypt. When Aziru does send them Yanhamu stops them on the way. Aziru asks the king to order Yanhamu to let Aziru's messengers get through. Of course, I realize this begs the question of how did this letter get through in the first place? One possibility is that he might have sent it with one of the King's personal commissioners who was rotating through the area.

Apparently Aziru has returned from Egypt safe and sound, unfortunately we have absolutely no idea of what transpired while he was in Egypt.

Reviewing the Aziru corpus we walk away in a state of confusion and frustration. At the end of this back and forth between the Pharaoh and Aziru about his returning to Akhet-Aten we still have no idea why the Pharaoh was adamant about Aziru visiting the palace.

Assuming that Rib-Hadda's letters are factual, which for the most part they appear to be, Aziru is fomenting trouble, assassinations, and insurrection. However, in Aziru's letters there isn't a whisper about Rib-Hadda, instead he constantly deflects to the fact that the Hittites are in the area and threatening to attack. So how credible is this threat?

Well evidently the king grew tired of these conflicting reports and apparently sent out three independent inquiries to investigate the Hittites activities (EA 174, 175, 176 and possible EA177) and three different kings claim that not only have the Hittites and set the cities on fire but that the Hittites had been assisted by Ettakama the King of Kinsa!

Ili-Rapih

EA 140   Ili-Rapih's letter appears to have been written after the death of Rib-Hadda and it was definitely composed after Aziru had been recalled to Egypt and then left to return to Ammuru. As such this is one of the thought provoking letters yet. To start with he asks why does the Pharaoh communicate through Aziru? To show his astonishment at this IL-Raphih details that Aziru has systematically killed the King of Arduna, the King of Irqatta, the King of Ammiya the King of Ardata along with an unnamed magnate. Assuming this is correct and there's been little to dispute it, Aziru is beginning to look like the Charlie Manson of the mid-east. This is even more amazing because we know from Aziru's correspondence that the majority of it consisted simply of childish excuses justifying why he couldn't come to Egypt, they rarely rose above the level of "the dog ate my homework". Unsurprisingly there isn't a single reference in Aziru's letters about any of the kings that he supposedly murdered and by extension there isn't a single inquiry from Akhenaten about the various kings that Aziru was accused of murdering. This is kind of amazing because if I were the king of Egypt, I would be intensely interested whether I was recalling a serial murderer of kings to appear in my court; after all I might become the next victim.

Il-Rapih continues in his letter stating that even while Aziru was in Egypt, he continued his attack on the neighboring kingdoms sending his forces into Itakamma and the lands of Amqu.

Finally in the closing sentence it looks like the Hittites are active in the area but alas it breaks off before we can get a complete report.

Abi-Milku

Abi-Milku was a commissioner for the king, and therefore further up the bureaucratic staircase than either Rib-Hadda or Abdi-Asirta were.

EA 146 ABI-MILKU The problem with this letter is that most of it is factually worthless. The majority of the letter is little more than Abi-Milku slobbering all over Akhenaten's feet as he praises him to the hilt. Once we finally wade our way through this Mississippi river of sugar-coated tripe, (in which to hear Abi Milku tell it), Akhenaten is the sun, the moon, the earth, nay he is the very firmament on which the entire universe rests comfortably, and said universe would collapse instantly without Akhenaten's divine grace constantly maintaining it. We finally get to an extremely fragmented description of his problems and they are; Zimredda is evidently attacking him and his cities and Zimredda and has cut off Abi-Milku's water supply and finally he says that the Apiru are also attacking various cities.

The Egyptian scribe held the latest clay tablet from Abi-Milku and began to read it. "To the King, my lord, my god, whose feet rest on the firmament created by his sacred father so that all life on earth could come out and bask in the warm glow of his majesty's presence. Every man, every woman, turns their head and listens with joy as their lord and master speaks to them. Their eyes light up as they listen very closely to every word of wisdom that you impart to them. He gives them the breath of life, he gives them the water they drink, he gives them the food they eat, he sustains them with every step they take…" the scribe took a deep breath exhaled and waited a moment hoping the pharaoh would give some hint that the scribe was supposed to either speed it up or stop. The Pharaoh was impassive but made the slightest nod of his head to his prime minister. The prime minister spoke. "We are all the gracious subjects of his majesty but tell us what Abi-Milku wants."

EA 147   After reading this letter I became firmly convinced that if they handed out Nobel prizes for the most nauseating sycophantic, factually worthless letters written in history Abi-Milku would instantly win it. Unsurprisingly, the majority of the letter consists of him praising the Pharaoh to the heavens and beyond, without ever once telling us what it is that he wants.

In fact, it's literally in the closing sentence of the letter that Abi-Milku spells out the fact that Zimredda writes daily to Aziru about all of the events going on in the Levant and Egypt and that the king should be aware of that fact.

EA 148   In this letter, for some reason Abi-Milku finally, mercifully dispenses with the avalanche of flattery that he had previously buried both us and the pharaoh in, and shifts to a more utilitarian and telegraphic style. Evidently the Pharaoh sent him a letter instructing him to start at the point, and get rid of the useless flattery. Instead, Abi-Milku confirms that he has sent an order of glass to the Pharaoh. After that Abi Milku makes an oblique reference to the Pharaoh returning a man named Usu to Abi Milku.

Abi-Milku then asks for 10 palace attendants to guard the city so that Abi-Milku can visit the Pharaoh. However, in a classic case of 'talking past the close', he also says, every day the King of Sidon has kidnapped one of Abi-Milku's palace attendants. Personally, this makes me wonder why would the king send ten men, to Abi Milku when they would undoubtedly be kidnapped? But alas that question is neither asked nor answered. Instead, he reiterates his desire to have Usu returned to him so 'he can fetch water and straw' i.e., get supplies for Abi-Milku. Clearly Usu is more important than just being a simple servant but alas we don't know what it is.

EA 149   In this letter we get an insight into how the message system works since Moran quotes Abi Milku as saying he wrote an *express* tablet (Moran EA 149 6-20) but obviously the king hadn't answered it. This shows that as commissioner Abi Milku must have had riders who knew the fastest routes back to Akhet-Aten and as such they might have had special privileges along the way. So, clearly this tablet had to be a follow-on report to the first one that is, as usual lost to us.

In this letter he asks that 20 palace attendants be sent to him so that he may see the king. Then after that Abi-Milku makes the subtly cynical comment that these men will be absolutely expedient. How do we know? Well, he rhetorically asks, what are their lives compared to the kings, and that if they die then they will live forever in the king's name. That's hardly a ringing endorsement for something that sounds like it will be a one-way suicide mission for the men. Fortunately, from the subsequent letters from Abi Milku it looks like this request was denied.

EA 150   In this letter Abi Milku has streamlined his opening comments down to the standard 'throwing himself at the king's feet seven times and seven times' format. Apparently, the negotiations for his return to Egypt are continuing. In the beginning he was asking for 10 then 20 palace attendants in exchange for him visiting the pharaoh, but he has now dropped his demands for a single soldier.

After that he pleads for Usu who it appears is being held prisoner by the Pharaoh to be released so that he may 'live and drink water'.

EA 151 Abi Milku continues with his abbreviated introductions the pharaoh. Unsurprisingly, the Pharaoh is clearly demanding that Abi Milku return to Egypt, and as usual he avers. Only this time it isn't the Hittites who are standing in the way. No, it's Zimredda of Sidon. Evidently Zimredda discovered that Abi Milku had been ordered to Egypt and promptly declared war on Abi Milku. In closing he asks for 20 men to guard the city so that he can return to Egypt.

He tells the king that they are located on the sea and have neither water nor wood and so Abi-Milku sends a gift of 5 talents of bronze, mallets, and wood.

Finally, he responds to the king's request to tell him what is going on in Canaan by informing him the king that the king of Danuna has died, and his brother is now the king. In addition to that a fire destroyed the palace at Ugarit.   The ubiquitous Hittite troops have magically disappeared. Ettakama and the ever-present Aziru are at war with Biryawaza. The ever-malignant Zimredda has apparently formed an alliance with Aziru and might be preparing an invasion. And in closing he says that the palace attendants are terrified of the impending war.

EA 152 In this letter Abi-Milku cuts straight to the chase that Zimredda, the ruler of Sidon, is at war with him. Abi-Milku now asks for 80 soldiers and provisions. Unfortunately, the tablet is so fragmentary that it's impossible to determine the rest of its contents.

EA 153   In this letter we get an aspect of how ruthless Abi Milku can be. The king has apparently ordered Abi-Milku to hold ships for the king's troops. And Abi-Milku complies with the request by saying that anybody who has disobeyed those orders was put to death along with their entire families.

EA 154   In this letter it is evident that the king's troops had arrived via the ships that were sequestered in the previous letter and as a result of this they put a stop to Zimredda's incursions. But in the time-honored tradition of the mid-east the moment the Pharaoh's troops left Zimredda instantly renewed his offensive against Abi-Milku and Sidon and as a result he has killed one man and captured another while still preventing the people from gathering wood or getting water.

EA 155 Abi Milku has finally found the right blend of flattery and learned how to mix it diplomatically with the facts. Especially when it is clear that the unnamed commissioner that he answers to is doing everything he can to undermine Abi-Milku's authority. In this case the king has ordered that provisions be given to Abi-Milku and just as clearly the unnamed commissioner is disobeying the orders and attempting to starve Abi-Milku into submission.

And then in closing Abi-Milku appears to be instigating a fight when he tells the king to inquire whether Sumur has been rebuilt. There seems to be an unwritten accusation, that Sumur still hasn't been rebuilt. He then makes an oblique reference to the fact that the mayor of Beirut is sending in one ship, while the ruler of Sidon is sending in two ships, Abi-Milku tops all of this by saying that all of his ships are at the king's disposal.

Chapter 11

If You Can't Harvest the Crops; Harvest the Peasants

EA 68   *Rib-Hadda looked out at the long empty plain that stood in front of the town of Sumur, and waited in anticipation for the next events to unfold. He knew that Abdi-Asirta and the Apiru were hiding in the hills watching him like wolves waiting for the shepherd to take his eyes off his flock; and when that happened, they would attack in the middle of the night. There was no telling when or where that treacherous dog would attack, there was just the certain knowledge that Abdi-Asirta would attack.*

But that was just one of Rib-Hadda's problems; among others were the fact that the king had sent an emissary named Appiha to Gubla, and now Rib-Hadda had to make sure that the man's every needs were met, lest he find fault in Rib-Hadda and report that to the king. The only thing that had happened during the man's stay was that the people were so outraged by what was transpiring around them that they ripped the bronze gates off the city.

But things were getting worse in neighboring Irqata that the Apiru led by Abdi-Asirta had killed their king.

Their attacks had become increasingly bold in the previous months, but each time they were successfully repelled. But that was just one of his concerns, Rib-Hadda's thoughts kept returning again and again to the fact that his Majesty the King, the giver of all life to his subjects, had for unknown reasons turned his back on his subjects and pulled the Egyptian garrison that had been guarding the city out of the country abandoning Rib-Hadda to his fate. Rib-Hadda remembered how he had watched in dismay as the troops had hitched up the horses to their chariots, and after that the archers climbed on board. Within an hour the 400 men had departed for Egypt, leaving him alone to face the onslaught of the enemies that now surrounded him...Rib-Hadda's scribe coughed gently in an attempt to get the mayor's attention. After all the clay was wet and drying quickly in the hot desert sun. The scribe sprinkled some water on the tablet to keep it moist. Rib-Hadda was still deep in thought, so the scribe coughed again, only louder this time, Rib-Hadda snapped out of his reverie and looked at the scribe with his stylus poised over the wet clay waiting to write the letter. Then Rib-Hadda began to dictate "Say to the lord my sun, the great king of the lands" Rib-Hadda continued with the florid torrent of words that were an absolute necessity in any communication with the king. That night Rib-Hadda sent his tablet by messenger to Akhet-Aten and waited patiently for a return. In the meantime, he continued to wait for Abdi-Asirta and the Apiru to make their next move against him.

But in the meantime, he needed money and supplies, and the answer was obvious; he would sell some of the peasants and their household goods in the land of Yarimuta.

A week later the peasants woke up to the thundering roar of the horses' hoofs pounding the ground outside their homes. Before long they heard the muted cries of the people as the soldiers barked orders back and forth. The man came out of his hut and looked on as his neighbor's son and daughter were seized by the troops. They were then bound by the hands and led to a cart that contained other sons and daughters of the village. Standing next to each cart was a scribe and his attendant as each person was brought to the cart. The scribe would take the person's name and age down and mark it on one of his clay tablets. Other soldiers would take chairs, tables, spoons, pots, and pans, and any tools to other accountants who would inventory the items they had received, who their owners had been and where they were to be sent to.

While all this was going on other soldiers were ransacking the peasant's homes. Tables and chairs vanished, pottery and bronze pans, family heirlooms were all confiscated to be sold.

It was an unshakeable law of the universe that empires were guarded by warriors, and run by accountants to make sure that the wheels of society continued to turn.

And towering above them all supervising the pillaging like a lion watching vultures tearing a corpse to pieces, was Rib-Hadda, the lord of the town. In a loud voice he announced to them "His majesty the king of Egypt has withdrawn the breath of life from Gubla. He has found it fitting not to respond to our needs for the time being. However, the city of Gubla needs supplies but we have none. Therefore, you and your sons and daughters will be sold into slavery along with all of your possessions in the land of Yarimuta. This will last until at such time as his lord and majesty sees fit to take cognizance of our dilemma."

And then he left…

The one thing that is clear from this first epistle is that Rib-Hadda is already in dire straits. To begin with he's sick whether from disease or exhaustion isn't made clear. But Rib-Hadda's health will come into play in further letters.

However, the reasons for his concern are immediately revealed to us; predictably the ubiquitous Apiru are waging a war against Rib-Hadda which he describes as severe.

How 'severe' is it? Well, Rib-Hadda states that the sons and daughters of the city have been sold in Yarimuta in order to buy provisions for the beleaguered city.

After that, things take a darker turn; it seems that the Apiru, are not only waging war against Rib-Hadda, but they have also killed Aduna the king of the Irquata. Unsurprisingly this assassination was according to Rib-Hadda apparently coordinated by his eternal nemesis Abdi-Asirta.

Evidently Adbi-Asirta wasn't alone in expanding his micro-empire in the Levant. Rib-Hadda calls attention to the fact that another ruler named Miya has just seized the city of Ardata. And if that isn't bad enough, then just to compound Rib-Hadda's problems he notes that the men of Ammiya had just revolted and killed their lord.

All in all, things weren't looking good for Rib-Hadda.

EA 69 *Four months had passed since Rib-Hadda had sent his last clay tablet to the Pharaoh at Akhet-Aten and he still had not received an answer. Rib-Hadda gazed out at the desolate courtyard of his palace and looked out at the empty entrance that had been adorned with a pair of beautiful bronze gates. The gates had simultaneously proclaimed the wealth of Gubla and prevented people from entering the palace. But now they were gone; having been ripped off their hinges by a mob of people who then carried them away to the hills undoubtedly to be melted down and turned into more weapons which in turn would be used to attack him.*

The Apiru's attacks were now becoming bolder and more relentless as they attacked both during the day and night. Rib-Hadda's situation was deteriorating on an almost daily basis. The towns that had been entrusted to Rib-Hadda to govern were now wavering in their support of him. Other cities such as Magdalu and Kuasbut had already joined the Apiru and Abdi-Asirta and then aligned themselves against Rib-Hadda.

The scribe was growing impatient; this time in order to get his Lord's attention he made a soft scratching noise with his stylus against the wooden table. Rib-Hada noticed the sound and began dictating his latest message to the King. "Say to the king 'Rib-Hadda I fall at your feet seven times and seven times'..."

Even though EA 68 and 69 have similar topics. We begin to notice subtle changes in them. For instance, any mention of the commissioner has vanished. On the other hand, the Apiru have apparently stepped up their attacks and are now according to Rib-Hadda attacking around the clock.

Interestingly, in this letter there is a reference to the arrival of a man named Appiha. Unfortunately, we don't know who this person was or why he had been dispatched to see Rib-Hadda, but he had clearly been sent by Akhenaten on some sort of surveillance mission. The only thing we know for certain is that during his stay something happened that infuriated the populace so much that it caused the citizens to rip off all of the bronze gates of Rib-Hadda's residence. Evidently Rib-Hadda knew that this would sound as unbelievable to the Pharaoh as it does to us, and anticipating the pharaoh's disbelief he urges the king to ask Appiha about it.

In a situation like that there are always a plethora of questions, starting with what happened to the gates? Who tore them down and why? After all bronze gates would be worth a substantial amount of money even in today's society of mass production, one can only imagine what they were worth back then.

Next what was Appiha's version of this event? Unfortunately, we have no idea. As usual the historical record is infuriatingly silent whenever we get to the interesting parts.

The only thing that is apparent is that civil chaos is ensuing at Sumur.

At the end of the letter Rib-Hadda closes with a request for more archers. More than likely this request was denied.

EA 70   In this short letter Rib-Hadda in his usual manner makes a plaintive attempt to have more archers sent to Ammuru.

EA 71 *Rib-Hadda gathered his thoughts regarding what to do about the never-ending problem of the Apiru. Since the palace wasn't responding to his letters it was time to take a different approach. Instead, he sent a letter to the commissioner Haya about the straits he was in. Hopefully he would listen to Rib-Hadda and then relay the urgency of the situation to the king, who would at last send some troops to fight Abdi-Asirta.*

Who is Haya? Alas, all we know of Haya is from the Amarna letters and predictably the letters are infuriatingly silent on what his exact position is within the hierarchy. It's safe to say that even though Haya was, far above Rib-Hadda in the bureaucracy, but well below the Pharaoh. The internal evidence from the letters suggest that he is some sort of free-floating emissary who might be described as 'the eyes and ears of the king'. In this position he would hopefully provide his majesty with a more objective account on what was going on in the empire.

Rib-Hadda in his usual binary way, at first attempts to flatter Haya by telling him he is a wise man, and then in the next sentence chastises him by asking him why he hasn't told the king about Rib-Hadda's dire straits? After that he expands on this theme by complaining about the fact, that as usual Abdi-Asirta is taking more of the king's cities and the king is, of course doing nothing to stop it. But that's just the beginning of Abdi-Asirta's treachery. Rib-Hadda complains that Abdi-Asirta is still continuing to align himself with the Apiru using them as auxiliary forces in his attacks on the various towns. Next, Rib-Hadda says that in order to counter these aggressive moves on Abdi-Asirta's part Rib-Hadda says that he needs 200 archers and 50 pairs of horses.

It's obvious that Haya didn't ask the Pharaoh to send more troops to Rib-Hadda and Rib-Hadda's attempt at an end run failed.

EA 72 is lost

EA 73   *Abdi-Asirta was more emboldened than ever. So far, the king hadn't sent out any troops to suppress the insurrection that Adbi-Asirta was leading. He clearly was tightening his grip on the Levant by intimidating the remaining mayors with threats to either join him or the face the consequences of disobedience; which was death. He then sent a letter to the leader of the city of Ammiya urging them to kill their leader then join him and the Apiru and be safe from any further retaliations.*

Rib-Hadda looked at the various letters he had received from his fellow mayors along with the news from spies that he had placed in other towns. The messages from all of them were dire. Unsurprisingly Abdi-Asirta and the Apiru were on the move raiding villages of supplies, holding up caravans and in general disrupting the normal ebb and flow of the Levant. Rib-Hadda already knew from other channels of communications that the mayors wanted Akhenaten to send more troops and archers to crush Abdi-Asirta but so far nothing had happened, and as a result Abdi-Asirta was free to continue his machinations which he did with impunity.

Rib-Hadda had already written to General Ammanapa's to see if he could use his influence at the palace to have the pharaoh send troops and archers. But unsurprisingly, as usual, nothing had happened. It was time to write a follow up letter and see if he could stir the general to action. He turned to his scribe and said "Begin writing. 'To Ammanapa, my father...'"

This letter is obviously a follow up letter to a previous letter that Rib-Hadda had written to General Amanappa requesting troops. From this letter's contents it's fairly easy to determine that the first letter contained the actual request for troops. Another interesting point is that since Rib-Hadda doesn't refer to any letters that Ammanapa sent to him in reply then more than likely Ammanapa ignored the first letter and never answered it.

But this doesn't stop Rib-Hadda from reiterating the contents of what was probably in the first letter because, he makes the chilling warning that Abdi-Asirta is trying to undermine the city of Ammiya by urging the men there to kill their mayor.

Rib-Hadda then closes with his typical request for more troops.

And from the subsequent letters its appears that the request was denied.

E.A. 74   Abdi-Asirta looked out over the dusty plains at the town of Sigata. Then he waved his hand, and his army allied with the Apiru swept down on the unsuspecting town like a plague of locusts descending on a field of wheat. Within hours the town fell to Abdi-Asirta and his army.

Like a microscopic god-king Abdi-Asirta looked on his accomplishments with pride. Up until now he was the lord of a tiny fiefdom. But with each conquest it was turning into the nucleus of a kingdom and before long he would be able to split free from Egyptian hegemony and once that happened, he would join the great powers of the world as an equal. But that moment still lay in the future. Today he had to deal with the ever-annoying Rib-Hadda. The man was like a cockroach, no matter how many times you tried to step on him, he kept escaping and then hiding in another corner only to emerge once the sun went down.

Rib-Hadda considered the latest news concerning Abdi-Asirta's invasions. The town of Sigata had fallen to Abdi-Asirta and now he had sent his agents in to undermine Ammiya.

The mayor of Ammiya could hear the gathering of men in the distance. It was the sound of his death approaching him. The rebels burst into his palace and beat and stabbed the palace guards to death. Then like wolves in pursuit of a crippled lamb they chased Ammiya through his residence. Bronze daggers appeared like angry hornets as the men pinned him to the ground and stabbed the screaming mayor to death. Then his dead his body was dragged into the courtyard and dumped there for all to see.

Abdi-Asirta looked on with pride at his latest accomplishment, Ammiya had fallen like a fresh fruit from the tree and into his hand. "Now there will be peace." He declared to all who were present.

A couple of days later Rib-Hadda heard about the fall of Ammiya and turned to his scribe and said "Begin writing" The scribe picked up his stylus and began to write. Rib-Hadda dictated "Rib-Hadda says…"

Rib-Hadda opens this letter with the lament that Akhenaten has evidently withdrawn his support from the city. This time he beseeches the Pharaoh to inspect the tablets of his father's house (i.e., Amenhotep III) to find a time when Gubla was not loyal to the pharaoh.

Interestingly this rather trivial side remark gives us some insight into the dynamics of the mid-east. It's clear from this comment that there had obviously been an active correspondence between Rib-Hadda's predecessor. Unfortunately, this part of the archive has been lost to us.

Times are clearly tough though for Rib-Hadda since he bemoans the fact that the 'sons and daughters of the King' (aka citizens) have been sold in the land of Yarimuta for provisions. This is clearly an exaggeration; obviously he didn't sell everybody into slavery, if he had then the towns would be desolate and there would be nothing to take over. However, clearly somebody was being 'sold down the river' (to use that laconic phrase that American slaves used to describe one aspect of the slave business.) to buy provisions.

From our point of view, it might seem unbelievable that Akhenaten would abandon Rib-Hadda's citizens and let them be sold into slavery. After all, how could the pharaoh be indifferent to his subjects? Well, the answer is simple. As we've already seen from the graves of the common workers at Akhet-Aten compassion and mercy were not part of his personality. So, given this grim observation it's hardly surprising that Rib-Hadda's appeal to Akhenaten obviously fell on deaf ears.

Once that happened, events grew more dire for Rib-Hadda; evidently all of the mountain villages have now joined the Apiru. In fact, if Rib-Hadda is to be believed he is completely surrounded and only has Gubla and two unnamed towns left to his control.

But things just go from bad to worse. Apparently while all of this is going on, his arch enemy Abdi-Asirta, has taken the town of Sigurta for himself. Now that he's in control of that city, he urges the men of Ammiya to kill their leader. According to Rib-Hadda they follow through with this murder because he complains that the city is now like the Apiru.

But then the letter takes a strange happens after Abdi-Asirta gains control the city, Rib-Hadda writes that Abdi-Asirta wants the men to meet in the temple of Ninurta, and from there attack Gubla which is of course where Rib-Hadda resides.

When I read this, I wondered why Rib-Hadda drew attention to the fact that the meeting was in the temple of Ninurta? Why does Rib-Hadda feel the need to spell this out for the pharaoh? Well, it, turns out that ancient history, rests on an even much deeper layer of ancient history.

In this case I discovered that Ninurta was an early Sumerian god of farming and healing. By this time the Sumerians along with their language had long since vanished from the historical record. However, Ninurta had survived the death of the civilization he had risen from. During the ensuing millennia, he had evolved and become assimilated as a war god in the Assyrian pantheon. Clearly the reason Abdi-Asirta was assembling the men in the temple of Ninurta, the god of war, was both a psychological and spiritual ploy to turbocharge them into making an attack on Gubla and then finally disposing of Rib-Hadda for good.

The next question is of course, did Abdi-Asirta attack Gubla? And here's where we run into another frustrating dead end, and the answer is; we don't know.

EA 75   *Once again night settled gently on the town of Irqata, the town slowly settled down to its night time activities and the town slowly went to sleep.*

All except for several men dressed in black, they blended in with the few shadows that remained as they made their way to the king's palace in Irqata. They waited as bodyguards slowly changed positions or entered into conversations with each other and once they did the Apiru assassins moved past them and into the inner reaches of the palace. With hushed whispers and hand signs they took up their positions as one of them unsheathed his bronze dagger stepped out of the shadows and slit the king's throat with practiced ease. They waited until the body stopped convulsing from its death throes. For a few minutes they listened to the gentle stirrings of the night and then slipped out of the palace as silently as a snake sliding down a hole and vanished into the night entered.

Meanwhile Abdi-Asirta continued to wage against the hapless Rib-Hadda who continued to write to the palace and continued to receive nothing in return for it.

In other parts of the Levant. Miya the ruler of Arsani gathered his men together. He had watched how had Abdi-Asirta had captured the towns of Rib-Hadda like a peasant collecting the low hanging fruit from a neighbor's tree. If Abdi-Asirta, did it, why shouldn't he?

However, Abdi-Asirta's growing power worried some of the weaker powers in the Levant. Then in the town of Ammiya, Abdi-Asirta had slipped agent provocateurs. The agents had led a slow drumbeat urging the men of Ammiya to kill their lord, and finally after much vacillating a group of men had broken into the palace and beat him to death. And now the city had joined Abdi-Asirta.

But things were continuing to go downhill for Mitanni. The king of Mitanni continued to lose his grip on his vassals. The Hittite General Luppaku had now marshalled his army of 90,000 men around the capital of Mitannia. And then like a hurricane Suppiluliumas swept in with his army and chariots and had taken control of those territories for himself.

In his usual repetitive manner Rib-Hadda says that the war against him is severe and that the Apiru are attacking. And just in case the Pharaoh missed it the first time, he reiterates that the sons and daughters have been sold in Yarimuta for provisions.

However, in this letter there is a slight change in tone and it became intensely personal for a moment as Rib-Hadda mentions that he is suffering from some kind of illness, but whether this is physical or emotional isn't spelled out.

It's clear that the murderous Apiru are on the move again. On a much more sinister note, in this letter Rib-Hadda spells out the fact that the Apiru have recently killed Aduna the king of Irquata and nobody said a thing to stop Abdi-Asirta from continuing his conquests.

But it isn't just Abdi-Asirta who is on the move, evidently things have taken a turn for the worse as Rib-Hadda mentions that another ruler named Miya has just seized the town of Ardata. Of course, the treachery doesn't end there, and Rib-Hadda also chronicles the fact that the men of Ammiya have just now killed their lord.

I wondered why Rib-Hadda had gone into detail about the king of Irqata having been killed by his own men? This suggests the fact that the Pharaoh was already well acquainted with what was going on in this corner of the world, and didn't need a long explanation.

If we look at this letter in isolation it appears that the city of Irquata has fallen to the Apiru and has now been isolated from Egyptian sovereignty. The problem is that when we get to EA 100, we find the people of Irqata are sending a long letter to the Pharaoh swearing their undying allegiance to him. Another point is that with this we can reconstruct a part of the lost Pharaoh's letter to them in which he apparently demanded an unspecified amount of silver, along with 30 horses probably as tribute. The fact that Irqata delivered this to him without question shows that the Pharaoh's power had not diminished in the slightest in this region.

However, in my opinion the most critical piece of information is the fact that Rib-Hadda says that Suppiluliumas has now made his move against the Mitannians and has seized all the lands of the Mitanni, he notes that Suppiluliumas is now king of Nahrima, which is the Egyptian name for Mitanni.

EA 76   *Rib-Hadda reflected on everything that was going on around him. The war against him was relentless Abdi-Asirta was continuing to form alliances with the shadowy Apiru. Rib-Hadda shook his head in bewilderment. How could the King be so indifferent to his problems? Didn't he realize that even though they were at the very limits of the Egyptian empire that these threats could eventually threaten Egypt herself? In the past Egypt's kings ruled this area with an iron fist, but now the present king seemed to rule it with a fist of straw and appeared to be indifferent to the sufferings of his servants.*

Rib-Hadda called his scribe in and began dictating... "Say to the king..."

In this letter Rib-Hadda, with his usual monotonous predictability, complains that the war against him is severe. Rib-Hadda says that there are just two cities left to him. Then, just like clockwork, he states that Abdi-Asirta has gathered the Apiru for another attack on Sigata and Amp. He then complains that Sumur has joined the Apiru.

Rib-Hadda complains that in the past the king sent archers to make sure that he maintained control of his cities, but now for reasons that he didn't understand the Pharaoh had ceased that practice. In closing Rib-Hadda asks for a garrison of 400 men.

The fact that Rib-Hadda mentions that in previous times the pharaoh apparently had a rotating contingent of archers patrolling the borders of the empire suggests several things. Evidently these territories had been carefully monitored in previous years, but that practice had been abandoned.

The question is why?

I think the answer is rather simple: money. Rib-Hadda asked for a contingent of 400 men. By modern standards 400 men is a rather modest number, especially when we consider the fact that most invasions involve forces of a 100 thousand or more men, along with millions of tons of equipment. But we have to keep in mind that this isn't modern times, this is the bronze age and by our standards even the quickest lightning strike back then would take place at a snail's pace by today's standards of hypersonic missiles, and inter-continental rockets.

Clearly the cost to send, transport, and maintain 400 men across the desert to the far end of Lebanon must have been an enormous outlay of money and the return would have been insignificant. Given these rather dismal economic facts the Pharaoh had to assess what exactly would be his return on investment? To start with a horse has to eat 2 percent of its body weight per day. So doing the calculations, four hundred horses will eat 8,000 pounds of food a day, and that's if they're just standing there doing nothing. After that they each drink about 10 gallons of water a day for a total of about 4,000 gallons of water! The moment you hook them up to a chariot with a driver and then put an archer on board along with all of the gear needed to manage a horse, that number would increase dramatically. So, what did the Pharaoh's get in return? Well, the few letters to the vassals are usually orders for goods and services such as glass, women, and silver. Given these rather paltry requests for goods it seems unlikely that Akhenaten could hardly justify sending a contingent of 400 men and horses to Northern Lebanon.

Turning to his nemesis Abdi-Asirta, Rib-Hadda states that the Apiru are preparing to attack the cities of Sigata and Ampi. Not only that but he has also seized other towns whose names have been lost to us but he says that Sumur has joined the Apiru. He finally closes with his perpetual request for the king to send a huge number of archers to defend the city. In closing Rib-Hadda asks (apparently sarcastically) if Abdi-Asirta is the King of Mitanni or the King of Kassu.

EA 77 *General Amanappa fumed as he read the letter he had received from Rib-Hadda. Originally, he had ordered Rib-Hadda to deliver a certain amount of copper. Normally any other Mayor would have sent the copper immediately and along with it a note assuring him that this was the finest copper in the world.*

But that was what other mayors would do. Rib-Hadda, on the other hand, as usual marched to a different drummer on a meandering path that wandered off over a cliff.

No, instead of receiving the delivery of copper Ammanapa had ordered he received a clay tablet filled with excuses. Ammanapa quickly read the tablet to see what Rib-Hadda's latest reasons were for not delivering the precious metal.

This letter is different from the others by the fact that it is in response to another letter that was sent by General Ammanapa asking Rib-Hadda for copper.

In most letters when a demand for goods is sent to a subordinate the vassal the vassal, like a well-trained dog, usually responded that everything would be sent instantly. And then, perhaps to curry favor, the subordinate also assures the king that he will be astonished at the quality and quantity of the goods being sent.

Unsurprisingly though, Rib-Hadda, being the contrarian that Rib-Hadda is, he unapologetically refuses to send the copper with the plaintive excuse that he had used it to buy supplies for his town. Then in his usual predictable manner, Rib-Hadda pivots using the rest of the letter as a springboard to complain about how dire his circumstances are and then closes with his usual request for more troops.

A request that was undoubtedly denied.

EA 78 This letter seems to be merely a recapitulation of EA 77.

EA 79 *Rib-Hadda stood before the scribe that was waiting for his lord to begin dictating another letter to the king. Recently the King had sent General Ammanapa to survey the situation and from there give him a full report on the situation in the Levant. The general had arrived with a small contingent of troops to guard him as he made his evaluation of the situation. And then left abruptly, without making any substantive decisions. What needed to be done next would be decided by the pharaoh and his advisors. Rib-Hadda was both frustrated and disappointed at this chain of events. Finally, Rib-Hadda took a deep breath and began dictating. "Say to the Lord my King..."*

In this letter that Rib-Hadda wrote to the king, it was apparent that he had sent General Ammanapa to investigate what the situation was like in the Northern Levant. Unfortunately, exactly what the general's orders were and what his findings consisted of are never revealed to us and, once again, we've hit another dead end in the Amarna Hall of Mirrors.

Another possibility is that after the General arrived Abdi-Asirta broke off his attacks against Rib-Hadda for the moment. And of course, the moment Ammanapa left, Abdi-Asirta promptly attacked the towns of Bit-arha. After they fell, they joined the Apiru, along with Abdi-Asirta. As a result of that he now had Gubla and Batruna in his sights.

In closing Rib-Hadda tells us that all of the Apiru, at the instigation of Abdi-Asirta, have turned against Rib-Hadda and then he closes with his usual lament that he is trapped like a bird in a cage.

EA 80 Lost message.

EA 81 *Rib-Hadda heard a faint noise in his room, he turned around and saw the man's silhouette against the wall, and then with breath taking speed the would-be assassin moved towards him with his dagger extended as he made a slashing strike at Rib-Hadda's throat. Instinctively Rib-Hadda pulled back before the knife found its target.*

It was clear that the Apiru might have been a practiced and experienced assassin, skilled at his craft, however he was up against an even more determined Rib-Hadda who was a world class survivor both in the cerebral world of politics and the physical world of fighting; as such his would be killer didn't stand a chance against him.

The assassin made another slashing motion and Rib-Hadda pulled back from the thrust, and avoided being killed, but not far enough, the knife cut into him slightly, the assassin rotated his knife 180 degrees and made a stabbing motion. Rib-Hadda dodged the parry but the knife still found its mark and bit into his side leaving a slight cut. Rib-Hadda could feel the blood trickling down his ribs. He was unarmed so he grabbed a chair and threw it at his would-be assassin. The man dodged it but moved in again and aimed low as he attempted a slashing motion at Rib-Hadda's legs. Rib-Hadda's thigh caught the tip of the knife and there was a slight wound. He pulled back staying clear of both the tip of the knife and the edge of the blade, while circling around trying to get inside and body slam the man. Rib-Hadda miscalculated and instead, the assassin struck him again slicing him in the arm. They continued the ballet of death as the assassin stabbed Rib-Hadda six more times, and then the man made a mistake. The assassin came into make a close parry and then slipped on Rib-Hadda's blood. It threw him off just enough that it allowed Rib-Hadda to close the gap as the knife went sailing past him. Rib-

Hadda bent his arm and slammed his elbow into the assassin's jaw. The pain shot through the assassin's face and head like an exploding lightning bolt, he struggled to keep his composure, but it was too late; Rib-Hadda finally grabbed the knife twisted it from the man's hand, reversed it and slammed the point deep into his would-be assassin's stomach severing a major artery. The assassin's body went limp in Rib-Hadda's arms, he let him go and watched as he slid to the floor dead. Rib-Hadda finally stood over the man's corpse, exhausted but alive.

Rib-Hadda had the body dragged out of his room, while other servants cleaned up the mess. The next morning Rib-Hadda summoned his scribe and began dictating. "Say to the King..."

Now that Abdi-Asirta's power is increasing he is urging the men of Gubla to turn against Rib-Hadda and kill him. Evidently, Abdi-Asirta's agent provocateurs have successfully infiltrated a man with a bronze knife into the palace who attempted to kill Rib-Hadda. The man nearly succeeds and after striking Rib-Hadda nine times Rib-hadda manages to kill the would-be assassin.

According to Rib-Hadda only Gubla and Batruna remain in Rib-Hadda's control. Evidently Abdi-Asirta has infiltrated Apiru agent provocateurs into the city to recruit fifth columnists and then urge the men of Gubla to kill Rib-Hadda.

Rib-Hadda then pleads for more archers saying that if they don't arrive within two months Abdi-Asirta and the Apiru will take the two towns remaining.

EA 82 *Rib-Hadda was furious by General Ammanapa's inaction. Abdi-Asirta and the Apiru continued in their attacks on him day and night. But Amanappa always had the same answer; he told Rib-Hadda to send a man to the palace to request more troops and as soon as the request arrived and been approved, then he Amanappa, will send troops to Rib-Hadda. Rib-Hadda had replied again and again that he was unable to send anyone one to the palace because the moment Abdi-Asirta found out about it Rib-Hadda's messengers were kidnapped.*

Rib-Hadda continues in his litany of complaints to and about Amanappa. He had ordered Rib-Hadda to send ships to the port of Yarimuta in order to export various goods. The problem was that the men Amanappa had sent to Rib-Hadda had run away as soon as they could and as a result there was no one to get the goods out.

In this letter Rib-Hadda writes directly to Ammanapa addressing him as 'Father'. However, it should be kept in mind that even though he calls 'Ammanapa' his 'father' and refers to himself as 'your son' this is undoubtedly a ceremonial description reflecting the difference in their ranks, and not an actual reference to any biological relationship.

Rib-Hadda takes a different approach in this letter; instead of appealing directly to the pharaoh for help, he asks why Ammanapa hasn't rescued him.

For reasons that are obscure Ammanapa had evidently told Rib-Hadda to send a representative directly to the king to plead his case. Then once the order came back from the king, Ammanapa would then send in the troops. Clearly, he was telling Rib-Hadda that there was a chain of command in place and if Rib-Hadda wanted troops, then he would have to go through the pharaoh first, and then the pharaoh would release the troops and Ammanapa would attack. However, it was obvious that Ammanapa was not going to violate or disrupt that chain of command.

Instead of doing the logical thing and following Ammanapa's instructions, Rib-Hadda protests, for unspecified reasons, that he can't send anybody to the palace. Apparently, Abdi-Asirta's spies are in place and are preventing Rib-Hadda's men from reaching the palace.

And then just to compound the matter apparently Ammanapa had also told Rib-Hada to send a ship to Yarimuta so that he can receive supplies. Rib-Hadda deflects again and says that all the men that Ammanapa had sent him have run away!

Rib-Hadda repeats the fact that he survived an assassination attempt and unsurprisingly makes the empty threat to abandon the city if he isn't rescued. The only thing that is clear is that Abdi-Asirta has the mayors completely cowed because according to Rib-Hadda, the moment the mayors hear anything they promptly report it directly to Abdi-Asirta.

In closing Rib-Hadda makes another threat to abandon Byblos unless he gets help. Finally, Rib-Hadda describes to Amannapa how he was stabbed 9 times in a previous assassination attempt.

E.A 83 *Once again Rib-Hadda had sent a letter to the pharaoh, and once again the Pharaoh hadn't answered it. Finally, after months of waiting for a reply and receiving none Rib-*

Hadda had grown impatient and sent out another man with the message. Unsurprisingly this messenger along with his horses vanished into the labyrinthine world that was Akhet-Aten. Evidently, they were being 'detained', after all 'kidnapped' was such an ugly word, and if it was used it would merely exacerbate the situation. Finally, after three months of waiting for a reply Rib-Hadda had grown tired of waiting and began dictating to his scribe "Say to the King my Lord..."

Once he was through, Rib-Hadda waited until night and then sent his messenger off with two horses, one horse to ride and another in reserve. He watched as the man galloped off toward Akhet-Aten and then waited for him to return.

In this letter Rib-Hadda wants to know why the king hasn't responded to his previous letters. Evidently, Rib-Hadda had sent a messenger to the king. Upon their arrival, for unspecified reasons, both the messenger and his horses were taken into 'protective custody'! Normally most people would take the hint, that the king clearly wasn't interested in you or your message, and dropped the matter. However, we have to keep in mind that we're talking about Rib-Hadda, who as we know by now is as tone deaf as a granite statue. So, Rib-Hadda being Rib-Hadda, sends a second man who was also apparently detained by the king. I'm sure at this point in time, any other mayor would have taken the hint after his first messenger was detained and his horses taken by the Pharaoh. After the second messenger was 'detained' then it should have been crystal clear to Rib-Hadda, and anybody on planet earth with an ounce of common sense, that for whatever reason, his Majesty wasn't interested in anything Rib-Hadda had to say.

But the rules don't apply to our clueless Rib-Hadda. Instead he sends a third man to the palace and this time he evidently makes it back to Rib-Hadda. So, if this reading is correct Rib-Hadda has evidently sent a total of 3 men and six horses to relay the same message to the king!

Whether it's hubris, or political insensitivity Rib-Hadda then demands a garrison of men and horses be sent to him. Then in his usual blundering manner Rib-Hadda makes the empty threat to desert the king if he doesn't get the troops then like Yapah-Hadda and Zimredda he will form an alliance with Abdi-Asirta. However, in his usual tactless way, Rib-Hadda fumbles on reporting that Sumur and Bit-arha have also defected to Abdi-Asirta, and then Rib-Hadda contradicts himself and says he wants to be placed under the commissioner Yanhamu. This of course neutralizes his initial threat to defect if the pharaoh doesn't send Rib-Hadda troops.

Finally, since he's on a roll, Rib-Hadda adds another item to his meandering wish list and demands that his messenger be released and returned to him since the man's family is very upset with Rib-Hadda.

And as usual we don't know how much if anything the Pharaoh granted him

EA 84 *Abdi-Asirta had assembled his army along with the Apiru and looked out over the plains at the city of Sumur. And then he motioned with his hand to begin the attack. Before long the defenders of the city were killed and had begun to fall back. The civilians scattered before them like leaves in front of a hurricane as Abdi-Asirta and the Apiru began invading the city. Within hours Sumur was in Abdi-Asirta's control.*

Then, in a sinister move, Abdi-Asirta sent more messages to the mayors who were cowed by him. "Tell the other's that the city of Gubla has fallen and I now control everything." The mayors, like well trained dogs did as they were told and spread the rumor that Gubla had fallen, until it finally reached Akhet-Aten.

Within a week, the fall of Sumur reached Rib-Hadda's. Rib-Hadda started dictating to his scribe "Say to the King my lord"…

Rib-Hadda reiterates that the city of Sumur has fallen to Abdi-Asirta. This so enrages Rib-Hadda that he launches into some colorful metaphors comparing Abdi-Asirta to a thief sleeping in the King's bed, who then rifles the King's treasure room and taking anything, he wants. Rib-Hadda wonders why the king doesn't stop Abdi-Asirta from pillaging his cities. Evidently Rib-Hadda thinks this heavy-handed attempt at man-shaming will move the Pharaoh to act; of course, it doesn't.

In this perpetually rewritten version of *The Gospel According to Rib-Hadda* the city of Gubla is still being retained by Rib-Hadda. But Rib-Hadda warns ominously that the city is threatened by Abdi-Asirta and as such is in danger of falling to him unless the king sends a strong commissioner to make sure that it stands.

In this letter it's clear that Rib-Hadda has received information that other mayors were trying to undermine him. They're doing this by reporting that Gubla has fallen to Abdi-Asirta which it evidently hasn't. Rib-Hadda denies that this has taken place and asks that a commissioner be sent along with troops to fight off Abdi-Asirta.

In a much more fragmented part of the letter evidently Rib-Hadda had evidently sent several people to Akhet-Aten, again for unspecified reasons. Whether this is the same group of people mentioned in EA 83 or a different group is never explained. This time Rib-Hadda mentions the people the Pharaoh is holding by name; a man named Abdi-Ninurta, a woman named Ummahnu and her husband Milkuru are all apparently being detained by Akhenaten for unknown reasons. Since the last legible word in the tablet is 'send' I think it obvious that Rib-Hadda wants them returned.

Unsurprisingly whether they were returned is never specified.

EA 85   *In the months that had passed since Rib-Hadda had last written to the Pharaoh his request to be placed under the mentorship of Yanhamu had been granted. However, things weren't going the way he had planned. The problem was that when he asked Yanhamu for grain. Yanhamu then told Rib-Hadda to deposit a certain amount of money with a man named Yapah-Hada to secure enough grain to feed forty men. Rib-Hadda had made the deposit and was patiently awaiting the delivery of grain. The only problem was the grain was never delivered. Apparently instead of sending the grain as he was supposed to Yapah-Hadda had vanished with both the money and the grain.*

As a result of this double-dealing an infuriated Rib-Hadda had written to Yanhamu demanding that Rib-Hadda should either get his money back or the grain should be delivered. But so far, nothing had happened. Unsurprisingly Rib-Hadda wrote a letter to the Pharaoh telling him about the situation, and asking him to consult with Puheya to get the complete story.

Rib-Hadda reviewed the situation; for two years now Abdi-Asirta had been conspiring against Rib-Hadda attacking him constantly. Already in this year alone there had been 3 attacks on Rib-Hadda. In one of them he had been robbed of his grain. Now, in order to purchase supplies, he had sold some of the peasantry along with their furnishings in the land of Yarimuta for provisions.

Rib-Hadda called his scribe in and said. "Say to the King my lord."

The scribe began to write down Rib-Hadda's message…

In this letter we can finally begin to put a time frame on how long the war with Abdi-Asirta has been going. Rib-Hadda says that it has been going on for two years, and that Abdi-Asirta has specifically attacked him three times during this year robbing him of his grain.

As the letter continues Rib-Hadda makes the plaintive cry of desperation, saying that he has sold the people and their furnishings in the land of Yarimuta for provisions. This gives us both an insight into Rib-Hadda's power as a leader and his ruthlessness, that he can sell his people into slavery with impunity, and also the pharaoh's utter indifference to the plight of his subjects in the Levant.

Next Rib-Hadda says that he needs 400 men and 30 pairs of horses in order to defend the city. He pointedly notes that this is the same number of men and horses that were given to the ruler Surrata. The unspoken statement of course is that if the pharaoh can send 400 men to Surrata he can easily send 400 men to Gubla.

Then Rib-Hadda was apparently the victim of an embezzlement plot. Just to recapitulate Rib-Hadda in EA 85 said that he had wanted to be placed under Yanhamu's protection with the hope that he would be given grain to survive. But that backfired disastrously. Even though he is nominally under Yanhamu's protection Rib-Hadda still hadn't received the grain that he had been promised. The problem is that he had deposited the money for the grain with a man named Yappah-Hadda who then in the finest tradition of larceny, kept both the money and the grain.

At this point the letter takes an interesting turn and we get some insight into the mechanics of commerce and possible embezzlement.   Anticipating a skeptical Pharaoh Rib-Hadda tells him to talk to Puh-heya and ask about the fraud that was perpetrated on him. Unfortunately, we don't know how this embezzlement plot turns out, but it appears that there was a kleptocracy alive and well in ancient times just as there is in present times.

Not only that but Abdi-Asirta and the Apiru have gone to Yapah-Hada to form an alliance.

And finally, the king of Mitanni has sent reconnaissance forces evidently probing for weak points in the Levant but was forced to turn back due to lack of water.

EA 86   This is another part of the subset of letters that Rib-Hadda wrote to Amanappa.

In this letter Rib-Hadda writes a letter to General Ammanapa about the war against Abdi-Asirta which is now in its third year, and protests against the theft of his grain. Reading between the lines it is clear that after Rib-Hadda had written his letter to the Pharaoh detailing the lost grain, and the Pharaoh had evidently ordered either Yanhamu or Yapah-Hadda to deliver the grain to Rib-Hadda. In the usual back and forth world of Akhet-Aten the case of the purloined grain was apparently handed off to

Amanappa who ordered the grain to be sent. Which undoubtedly led to another letter being sent from Amanappa to Rib-Hadda telling him that the grain should be arriving 'any day now'.

Instead, Rib-Hadda rebuts Ammanapa with a rhetorical question of *"Haven't you heard?"* which clearly indicates the grain hasn't been delivered.   After that in the next sentence, an unnamed servant (who just like a character from a play by Shakespeare) enters the picture to deliver the critical line that spins the play in a completely different direction. Only in this case the text infuriatingly breaks off before we find out what earth shattering and plot twisting news the servant had to say! Undoubtedly, it was some weasel explanation about why the grain hasn't been delivered but unfortunately, we'll never know for sure. And as usual we're left in the well-known darkness of the Amarna Labyrinth.

In it Rib-Hadda makes his usual request for 400 men and 30 pairs of horses to defend the city. Rib-Hadda apparently considered this a fair request since the city of Surata had also been granted the troops. Unfortunately, there's no evidence that any troops for Rib-Hadda were deployed.

One of the things that isn't fully understood in this time period is why there was an abrupt change in Egypt's alliance with Mittania. We know that Egypt's relationships with Mittania had been strong under Amenhotep III, but then for unexplained reasons these warm relationships cooled off then froze solid under Akhenaten. As a result, Akhenaten did nothing to stop the Hittites from crushing the Mitannians and taking them into their empire. The question is what happened to precipitate this change in diplomacy?

Part of the answer might lie in the fact that the Mitannian's appear to have been subverting Egyptian hegemony in the Levant. As a result of this subterfuge Akhenaten then withdrew his support from Mitannia which led to its eventual collapse. The faint evidence for this is the fact that in this letter Rib-Hadda cryptically says that a great deal of material is being carried away to Mittania.

On a different note, we also might get our first hint of corruption in the Egyptian government, until now General Ammanapa looks like a paragon of virtue, and loyalty to the pharaoh. But Rib-Hadda complains that the pharaoh had sent him thirty pairs of horses and that Ammanapa had kept ten pairs for himself! And then in the very next sentence, he asks that grain from Yarimuta be given to them. So evidently Ammanapa also controls the grain supply from Yarimuta.

EA 87 *Three months earlier Rib-Hadda had sent a man to Ammanapa, (who, at the time, was with the king), in order to request troops. The messenger plead his case before the Pharaoh who, as usual, listened in silence. After all it wasn't fitting for a god king to acknowledge a lowly mortal subordinate in any way. Instead, once the Pharaoh made his decision one of the pharaoh's secretaries gave Rib-Hadda's messenger the bad news, there would be no troops, no chariots, and no archers being sent to Rib-Hadda. However, Rib-Hadda was still supposed to be on his guard and defend the cities of the pharaoh.*

Rib-Hadda turned to his scribe and said "Take these words down. 'To Ammanapa'…"

This is obviously a reply to another letter, now lost, that Ammanapa had sent to Rib-Hadda in which Ammanapa told Rib-Hadda to send a letter to him requesting troops. Once that happened Ammanapa would ask the Pharaoh for troops which would then be sent to Rib-Hadda. Rib Hadda had apparently complied with the request and sent his man to Ammanapa who was at the palace and then as usual nothing happened. And unsurprisingly Rib-Hadda was left to slowly twist in the breeze.

I think it's fairly clear that this message had evidently been leaked to Abdi-Asirta. When that happened, he promptly sent his troops out, along with the feared Apiru. And, unsurprisingly, they promptly took control of the town of Batruna and were now surrounding the gates of Gubla.

EA 88   In this tablet we get an idea of the scale of the war that was taking place. Rib-Hadda states that the cities of Ardat, Irqat, Ammiya, and Sigata are all being attacked by Abdi-Asirta. Whether these attacks are simultaneous, or on a rotational basis is never specified. However, recently Abdi-Asirta has also taken Batruna and is now moving reinforcements up against Gubla.

In fact, Rib-Hadda says that the war against him is so severe that if troops aren't forthcoming, before long that he will be forced to evacuate the city.

Finally, he closes with wondering why the king of Akka is favored since the palace furnished him with a horse. Rib-Hadda then makes a similar demand that his messenger be granted a horse too.

EA 89   *In order to find a safe place for various members of his family Rib-Hadda had placed his sister and her sons in Tyre, where he had gone to negotiate an alliance with their mayor. Rib Hadda hoped that she and her sons would be safe from Abdi-Asirta and the Apiru. And then after he left the unthinkable happened; that night assassins sprang into her room, she looked up in horror as one of them swung a Hittite war axe at her head. She pointlessly tried to arm to block blow, but instead it broke her arm in two; she watched with stunned horror as her hand dangled in front of her face like a five-finger pendulum. And then the Apiru assassin swung the axe, this time, from the side splitting her skull in two splattering her brains all over her bed. Her young sons looked on in horror as their mother's corpse slumped to the floor with a wet thud. At first, they were paralyzed with fear and then they desperately tried to escape, but they were too slow, and were instantly struck down in quick succession as two other assassins slammed their knives into their stomachs and gutted them like fish in the market place. Then they turned to the next room where Rib-Hadda's young nieces were sleeping and quickly slashed their throats. The massacre continued unabated, as other assassins ran through the palace and caught up with the mayor, they tripped then pinned him to the floor and stabbed him repeatedly leaving him to bleed to death on the palace floor. And once they were through the men vanished into the night.*

In this letter Rib-Hadda says; *"I made connubium with Tyre"*, which means marriage. But who got married; was this a symbolic 'marriage' between two cities, or was it a marriage between two people? Reading further it appears to be a political alliance a 'marriage of convenience'. Rib-Hadda was seeking an alliance with Tyre.

Evidently Abdi-Asirta had discovered that this potential alliance was in the works, and ruthlessly had the mayor killed, along with Rib-Hadda's sister and her sons and daughters.

Rib-Hadda then tries to bait the King into attacking Tyre by telling him that the palace has fabulous riches in it which are his for the taking if the king would just attack the city.

Unsurprisingly, I'm sure that after reading this letter of treachery and murder that would rival Shakespeare's Macbeth the king wisely doesn't rise to the bait.

EA 90   *Word had come back to Rib-Hadda that the King of Mitannia was sending 'expeditionary forces' to probe for weaknesses in the Levant. So far, they had all been easily rebuffed, but still they were a cause for concern.*

In this latest chapter of *"The Lamentations of Rib-Hadda"* our hero gives us a monotonous review of all the times he has asked the king for troops to defend the various cities in his charge. And just as predictably how his requests had fallen on the deaf ears of pharaoh. Then just as surely as the sun rose in the east and set in the west, his jeremiads were ignored, and once that happened Rib-Hada would watch, in helpless, hand wringing despair, as said cities fell effortlessly into the hands of Abdi-Asirta.

Rib-Hadda then pleads for more archers saying that all of the cities have been joined to the Apiru then finally Rib-Hadda asks for 30 pairs of horses.

EA 91   *Rib Hadda read the tablet from Abdi Asirta had sent him which demanded that if Rib-Hadda wanted peace with him and the Apiru then he would have to pay him the extravagant bribe of 1,000 shekels of silver along with 100 shekels of gold.*

Rib-Hadda was desperate. He called his scribe and said "Write to the King..."

In this extremely fragmented letter Rib-Hadda reiterates that Abdi-Asirta, is again, on the march. He reminds the king that Sumur has fallen and that the king had done nothing to prevent its fall. As a result of this Abdi-Asirta is now confident in his abilities and is closing in on an attack of Gubla.

But things just kept getting worse. Abdi-Asirta is currently attacking Rib-Hadda's orchards; evidently preventing the harvest from taking place. This would be the modern-day equivalent of deforestation. Mutiny is in the air and as a result his men are beginning to turn against him.

One thing that does appear to be different is that Abdi-Asirta is clearly using some kind of back channels to communicate with Rib-Hadda in an effort to extort 1,000 shekels of silver and 100 shekels of gold. The message is clear; if the ransom is paid then he'll break off the attack. Rib-Hadda writes to the King asking him for the money. Of course, at this point it's fairly obvious to anybody who has read any of the Amarna letters knows that the Pharaoh isn't going to bend to these clumsy attempts at extortion. After all, the money moves in only direction from the vassal to the pharaoh, and never the reverse.

Rib-Hadda closes with his usual exhortation to send more archers which is of course denied.

EA 92   This letter is difficult to understand. To start with in the first part of the letter Rib-Hadda complains that he has sent his messengers to the king clearly requesting troops, and the messengers returned without a message or troops.

Apparently, Abdi-Asirta has discovered this interesting fact and, unsurprisingly, he begins an attack on Rib-Hadda's cities.

However, in the second part of the letter Rib-Hadda says that the pharaoh has finally taken note of Rib-Hadda's plight and that the Pharaoh has written letters to Beirut, Sidon, and Tyre ordering them to send reinforcements to Rib-Hadda. Finally, the pharaoh told the mayors that Rib-Hadda would be writing to them for the troops and that they should obey.

From the letter it is clear that Rib-Hadda has already sent his letters to the other mayors requesting the troops. But apparently nobody has gotten around to reading their clay-mail because so far, they haven't sent a single man to Rib-Hadda's aid. As a result of this Abdi-Asirta is continuing the fight against Rib-Hadda.

EA 93 This extremely short letter clearly belongs to the subset of letters that were sent from Rib-Hadda to General Ammanapa. In this one Rib-Hadda angrily demands that Ammanapa write to the king so that he can send 300 men to Rib-Hadda. Evidently Rib-hadda wants to take Batruna back since this will weaken Abdi-Asirta's grip on the Levant.

EA 94   In this rather general letter, and pointless letter Rib-Hadda takes a shotgun approach accusing everybody of treachery and as usual never spells out exactly what the treachcrous things are. Rib-Hadda has once again asked the king to send out archers and as usual the king hasn't sent them.

EA 95 In this brief but ominous letter Rib-Hadda documents the fact that the King of Mitanni has personally visited Ammuru and declared that it is vast and prosperous. The implied threat here is that the King of Mitanni is preparing to take the land for himself. Apparently, Rib-Hadda attempts to forestall this invasion by having the king sending him 200 troops.

Rib-Hadda closes by saying that Abdi-Asirta is ill and may be near death. Rib-Hadda speculates that nobody knows what will happens after Abdi-Asirta dies.

EA 96.   *General Amanappa read the message from Rib-Hadda. It was simply a reply to his letter inquiring why some men had not been allowed to enter Sumur. Rib-Hadda had written back that the men were denied entry into Sumur because according to Rib-Hadda, there was some kind of pestilence that had infected Sumur. Apparently several more letters went back and forth between the two men. During this time Rib-Hadda made his usual excuses as to why no actions had taken place.*

This is a fascinating letter if for no other reason than we get away from the never-ending plight of Rib-Hadda and Abdi-Asirta.

Even though the letter appears to deal with, (by our standards) the rather trivial and perhaps humorous matter of the king's asses. What makes this letter interesting is that in this case we can see, that this was originally part of a cycle consisting of at least six letters of which this is the only one we have.

The conjectured first letter was evidently from Ammanapa to Rib-Hadda asking why the men from Sumur were not allowed to enter Rib-Hadda's city. The second letter was from Rib-Hadda to Ammanapa explaining why he refused to allow the men into his city. In this case because it was of an unspecified pestilence that was attacking Sumur. This precipitated letter three, the letter that we have, from Ammanapa back to Rib-Hadda who skeptically asked what kind of pestilence this was; one that affected men or asses? He then orders Rib-Hadda to send men to guard Sumur. This in turn undoubtedly resulted in a lost fourth letter from Ammanapa being sent to Akhenaten describing the whole incident along with comments that he was awaiting instructions from Akhenaten on what to do. Once the king answered that would be a fifth letter, after which Ammanapa would undoubtedly write the sixth letter to Rib-Hadda about the King's displeasure.

The important thing here is that we get a brief insight into Rib-Hadda's duties. Evidently the king had a large herd of asses that were under Rib-Hadda's control, and feeding and taking care of the animals was undoubtedly part of his responsibilities. In our modern-day world, the extent of this responsibility is difficult to imagine, so instead just imagine if you were a modern manager and you were in charge of a fleet of a hundred high end trucks, and it's you're in charge of making sure the vehicles are in top mechanical shape at all times. But there's a caveat to your responsibilities; if something goes wrong with the truck the CEO of the company is going to hold you personally responsible for fixing it. Now factor into this scenario that there are rings of truck thieves trying to steal your trucks or vandalize them. And in addition to that you have a team of drivers who run the gamut from highly responsible to people who are working with the truck thieves to steal your vehicles.

EA 97   This is again one of those anomalous letters that keeps showing up in the archives. This is a letter from a man named to Summu Haddi from Yappah-Hadda.   Evidently the lands that had been entrusted to Yappah-Hadda had now fallen to the troops of Abdi-Asirta because of his relentless attacks that were taking place throughout the Levant. As a result, no one is safe from his raids. Commissioners were being killed, caravans were raided, and mayors were assassinated and unsurprisingly the Palace did nothing to stop it. But even though Yappah-Hadda had written to the Pharaoh repeatedly requesting more troops they had always been denied.

EA 98   This is another message from to Yanhamu from Yappah-Hadda, the same man that had earlier embezzled both the money and the grain from Rib-Hadda. Only this time he writes that Aziru is blockading Sumur, and asks Yappah-Hadda to ask for the palace for instructions on what to do.

EA 99   What makes this letter fascinating, is that this is one of the few times that we get a rare insight into the master/slave relationship that existed between the pharaoh and his subjects. In this letter (which had been broken so that the mayor's name was lost to us) the Pharaoh demands the following; first that the mayor is to prepare his daughter for the King and the contributions to accompany her; 20 first class slaves, along with chariots and first-class horses. In return for this generous gift the vassal gets absolutely nothing, except the good tidings that the king is hale and hearty like the sun and everything is fine at Akhet-Aten.

Although we don't know who this letter is directed to, the one thing we can be absolutely certain of is that it wasn't Rib-Hadda. Why do I say the recipient wasn't Rib-Hadda? Because the king knows what his reply would be: not less than ten thousand well-chosen words, explaining how it was impossible to meet the king's request because Rib-Hadda's chariots were broken, his slaves had run away, and his daughters either had a broken leg, or were busy fighting the Apiru. And then he would close the letter by demanding that the king send 100 men and 50 archers as soon as possible.

EA 100   Message from the city of Irqata The people of Irqata have written to Akhenaten to tell him that they are loyal to him. In the course of the letter the pharaoh is obviously asking about an event where they evidently gave silver to the people of Subaru along with 30 horses and chariots. This was an extravagant bribe of some kind. Not only that but the King had ordered them to raid the land of the Apiru and retake the lands that had been previously captured. However, they don't say whether they obeyed this directive or not. Instead, they ask for a gift from the king so that their enemies will see it and 'eat dirt'. They promise to keep the gates barred until the king arrives.

EA101 The *Mitannian assassin slipped into the city that night and made his way to Abdi-Asirta's residence determined to kill Abdi-Asirta. The problem was that Abdi-Asirta had failed to pay a debt to the king of Mitanni. And the now the king was seeking compensation for his loss; Abdi-Asirta would pay his debts off with his life. Originally the king of Mitanni had demanded wool, and linen, and the precious stone lapis lazuli that was coveted by the nobility. It had then come to the Mitannian king's attention that Abdi-Asirta was siphoning these precious items into his own pocket. That, of course, was not to be tolerated but had to be ruthlessly throttled; the vassals had to learn a lesson; they were all whimpering dogs of no consequence, they were the dirt beneath the feet of their lords and masters. And if they thought otherwise, they would be buried in the soil of their treachery. In the end their deaths would serve as a gentle reminder to their successors of the price that treachery carried.*

The assassin slipped past the guards and from there into Abdi-Asirta's bedroom. Once there he slammed on palm across Abdi-Asirta's nose and mouth to stifle any scream and plunged the knife into his neck. Abdi-Asirta's eye-lids flew open and for a brief second as he saw his assassin, and then in the next second he slipped into the eternal darkness of death. The assassin vanished like a shadow in the night never to be seen or heard from again.

In this letter we get the extremely abbreviated message that Abdi-Asirta has been killed. Unravelling this letter is extremely challenging, but a close reading of it suggests that the reason he was killed was that he failed to pay the correct amount of tribute to the men of Ammuru who in turn were evidently paying it to their Mitannian overlords.

Of course, this rather convoluted passage leads me to wonder if the Mitannians were busy extorting money from the land of Ammuru. The area was nominally under Egyptian control but I still wonder if they threatened the local leaders with military action if they didn't pay the tribute. This in turn led them to killing Abdi-Asirta for withholding funds. I realize that this sounds very Machiavellian (come to think of it is Machiavellian) and over-complicated. At this point one reaches for an argument in logic called 'Occam's razor'. In a nutshell 'Occam's razor' says that given two competing theories the one with the fewest variables, or assumptions is the one that's most likely to be correct. And generally speaking, this holds true. Of course, the weak point of Occam's razor is that Occam's razor just holds for *two* theories. But in the Amarna "Hall of Mirrors "nothing is what it appears to be and we have to consider any number of possibilities. I know this rather circuitous logic might sound strained, except when you read the Amarna letters and other documents your mind automatically goes in this direction.

The one thing that is clear is that Abdi-Asirta underestimated his opponent. The more laidback Akhenaten would have undoubtedly overlooked Abdi-Asirta's embezzlement. But the more hard-headed Mitannians obviously frowned on this activity. They took a different approach to those who owed them money and sent an assassin out to kill him.

Then for reasons that are opaque at this point in time we get an extremely cryptic sentence that the ships of the army are not to enter the land of Ammuru, because Abdi-Asirta has been assassinated. What was the cause for this warning? Apparently, it is the men of Arwada who are hijacking the ships.

From the very beginning Rib-Hadda has railed against the evil of Abdi-Asirta going into an almost day by day description of the man, and in the end, we get only the vaguest outline of what happened to him.

EA 102   Apparently, the king finally decided to act and he has ordered Rib-Hadda to go and stay in Sumur. But, as usual, Rib-Hadda says that they can't get to the city. Things are going downhill and now another city, Ampi is at war with him. However, the surrounding cities have made peace with the sons of Abdi-Asirta.

Rib-Hadda urges the king to arrive with all due speed assuring the pharaoh that once that happens the attack on the city will collapse and be returned to his power.

EA 103   *Rib-Hadda surveyed his options and they're narrowing with each day. Currently the sons of Abdi-Asirta were attacking him constantly. According to Rib-Hadda they now have occupied most of the land of Ammuru. Rib-Hadda controls only Irqata and Sumur. Rib-Hadda has left Gubla but Zimredda and Yappah Hadda were not with him.*

In his usual predictable manner Rib-Hadda pointlessly asks for a garrison to guard the city until the archers arrive. In addition, he also wants a garrison sent to Irqata to defend it. And then Rib-Hadda pointlessly asks for 20 pairs of horses. Unfortunately, Rib-Hadda, who is a master at talking past the close, says that the entire garrison has already abandoned Gubla, so clearly, any chances of getting the 20 horses has evaporated with that revelation.

E.A. 104   Rib-Hadda writes to the king that Pu-bahla the son of Abdi-Asirta has now occupied Ulassa. Abdi-Asirta's sons now control Ardata, Wahliya, Ampi, and Sigata. Rib-Hadda tries to man shame the Pharaoh by asking rhetorically if these brigands are the king of Mitannia, or Hatti. They have driven the commissioners out and have taken Ulassa.

They are going to take Sumur and after that kill the commissioner and the auxiliary force in Sumur.

Now the cities of Ampi, Ulassa, Erwada are at war with Rib-Hadda, and as a result he cannot enter Sumur.

EA 105   In this letter is a good survey of the problems that Rib-Hadda is dealing with. Currently, there is a two-pronged attack being conducted by the sons of Abdi-Asirta and the people of Arwada. In the first prong Abdi-Asirta is attacking by land, while the people of Arwada are blockading any shipping from Rib-Hadda. Rib-Hadda complains that he tried to send 3 ships to Yanhamu but they were intercepted by the people of Arwada.

Rib-Hadda then makes a historical reference to one of the times when the Pharaoh did send archers to the Levant and suppressed a revolt staged by Abdi-Asirta. Apparently as a measure of the Pharaoh's benevolence None of Abdi-Asirta's ships or their goods were taken and he was allowed to keep his possessions. The problem is that this policy of forgiveness failed and now Abdi-Asirta's sons have inherited his wealth and have now taken Ulassa and they strive to take Ulassa. A classic case of "no good deed goes unpunished."

Finally, Rib-Hadda notes that Yappah Hadda is at war with Rib-Hadda because of property that he stole from Rib-Hadda.

Some of the Egyptians that escaped Ulassa are now with Rib-Hadda but there is no grain for them to eat. Rib-Hadda cannot get his ships into Yarimuta because Yappah-Hadda is blockading the port and he cannot send them to Sumur because it is controlled by Arwada.

EA 106   Rib-Hadda says that Gubla is still a loyal city, and then says that he is the Pharaoh's "Foot Stool" this is the only time this metaphor is used.

The war for Sumur is severe and it has been raided up to the gates, but they have not been able to capture it.

Pharaoh asks rhetorically why tablets keep being sent to the palace and Rib-Hadda says because he is the most loyal of the king's mayors, he says he is not like Yapah-Hadda or Zimredda who have abandoned the king.

In this letter he specifically says the war against him has lasted for five years.

He wants Yanhamu the Parasol bearer to be sent to him and finally he wants 20 pairs of horses sent to him so that he can march against the enemies of the king.

EA 107   In this letter we discover one of the classic problems of all bureaucracies; after they grow to a certain size critical things are forgotten, mistakes are made. In current times guns are sent to one place and the ammunition is sent to another. Winter coats are sent to men in the desert, and air conditioners are sent to others in the arctic. This same problem seems to have occurred in ancient times too. In this case Rib-Hadda has charioteers to drive the chariots, but no chariots or horses for them to drive. So, in this letter he requests 30 pairs of horses along with the chariots.

Unsurprisingly, we don't know whether the King listened to his plea or not.

EA 108   In this letter Rib-Hadda describes how the sons of Abdi-Asirta have either stolen or won the king's horses and chariots in some unknown battle. Afterwards they sold both the charioteers and soldiers in the land of Subaru.

But then things are getting progressively worse, Rib-Hadda says all the messengers have to be sent at night to the palace lest Abdi-Asirta captures them.

Rib-Hadda predictably states that various people in the palace are lying about him and planting false rumors and, as usual, we have no idea what these lies are.

He closes the message with a request for 40 men to guard the city. In view of the fact that the sons of Abdi-Asirta had already kidnapped the charioteers, along with their horses and equipment it's hardly surprising that the king doesn't grant his request.

EA 109   Rib-Hadda opens with a reminder to the King that in previous times when the King of Mitanni attacked Egypt's vassals their ancestors did not desert them. But now when the sons of Abdi-Asirta are attacking Rib-Hadda the king does nothing, and as a result of this inaction Abdi Asirta and his sons have taken Ulassa. But, unsurprisingly, Rib-Hadda monotonously asserts his loyalty to the king and tells him that he expects the king will eventually come to the rescue.

However, as we progress in our story, we find that this wish is never fulfilled.

In their current attacks the sons of Abdi-Asirta have taken the king's chariots, charioteers, and soldiers but the king has done nothing to stop it. But it doesn't stop there. Abdi-Asirta's sons have now set the ransom price at 50 shekels of silver for the 12 men that were kidnapped. One man was apparently sold into slavery in Subaru. In a powerful metaphor Rib-Hadda says that previously when a man from Egypt arrived the people would cower, but now with the sons of Abdi-Asirta in control he makes the men of Egypt prowl around like dogs.

On a different note, Rib-Hadda says that he is unable to get a man from the palace into Sumur. Rib-Hadda closes with the plaintive note that all of his towns are at war with him.

And then he closes with the anticlimactic note that when Haya and Ammanapa departed with the copper and that they said that Rib-Hadda was a loyal servant.

EA 110   This fragmented letter deals with the ships of the army. However, we can at least discern that some of the ships had supplies that were supposed to be destined for Rib-Hadda and were probably hijacked. Evidently the mayors who were in control of the city have apparently given nothing to Rib-Hadda.

EA 111   In this fragmentary tablet we hear once again, another plaintive cry for more archers and if they aren't sent then all of the land will fall to the Apiru.

EA112   Rib-Hadda is obviously responding to a previous letter in which the king has made his obligatory demand for Rib-Hadda to guard the city night and day. And just as predictably instead of saying "*Oui, mon capitaine.*" as he should Rib-Hadda fires back with a sarcastic retort asking whether he should use his enemies or his peasantry to guard the city. He then asks the king to send him a garrison to guard the city. Rib-Hadda then reports that he smuggled Haya into Sumur in the middle of the night after he paid the Apiru 13 shekels of silver and a pair of mantles to accomplish the deed.

EA 113   *Yappah-Hadda looked on as the two ships that had been destined for Rib-Hadda had now been deflected to him instead. Yappah-Hadda's men swarmed on the ship and began taking inventory of everything that it contained.*

Rib-Hadda received the news that his ship had been waylaid. He called his scribe and said "Begin writing. Say to the King…"

Here we begin to see another aspect of Yappah-Hadda. For inexplicable reasons, Yappah-Hadda who had ostensibly been a friend of Rib-Hadda in earlier letters, but now has turned into an unforgiving adversary. In this letter Rib-Hadda has accused him of piracy in the seizure of two of his ships. Instead of taking the fight straight to Yappah-Hadda Rib-Hadda appears to be relentlessly legalistic and wants the king to send a commissioner to judge the crime. Interestingly he says the king can have everything if Rib-Hadda wins.

This raises an interesting question in morality; is Rib-Hadda telling the king he can have the winnings in an effort to bribe him or is Rib-Hadda saying that he only wants to be vindicated as the injured party and awards are of no interest to him?

In closing he asks the king why his messengers can't get through to the palace when other governors can. He wants Amananna to stay with him since that's the only way he can get his tablets through to the king.

EA 114   *Under the leadership of Aziru, the Apiru captured and bound 12 of Rib-Hadda's men who had been sent to guard Sumur. A few days later a clay tablet from Aziru was delivered to Rib-Hadda; demanding that he pay a ransom of 50 shekels in silver for the men, or else they would be sold into slavery. Rib-Hadda thought more and more about his desperate straits. Unsurprisingly Yappah-Hadda, the man who had stolen both his money and his grain in an earlier deal, had now joined forces with Aziru and the Apiru in the war against Rib-Hadda and had seized Rib-Hadda's ships. The war was getting severe as more reports came it that the men had abandoned Sumur.*

Rib-Hadda writes to the king that the war against him is severe. Aziru is still at war with him. Unsurprisingly he repeats the news that Aziru has seized 12 of Rib-Hadda's men and set the ransom price at 50 shekels. As usual, Rib-Hadda talks past the close and says that the men that the king has sent to Sumur were the ones that were kidnapped.

Aziru has tightened his grip on the area and has taken the port of Wahliya Rib-Hadda complains that the ships of the rulers of Tyre, Beirut and Sidon are peacefully stationed there.

Aziru is clearly succeeding in his effort to dominate Ammuru as he continues to seize the ships of Rib-Hadda with impunity. Unsurprisingly his peasants want to desert him but Rib-Hadda is still keeping them under control.

Rib-Hadda has urged the troops to defend Sumur but they have predictably abandoned their posts. Rib-Hadda says he has repeatedly sent messengers to Sumur, but all the roads have been blocked. He asks the king to evacuate him and if the king can't do that then send a contingent of archers to save him.

EA 115   Message lost

EA 116   Once again there was an attack on Rib-Hadda's garrison and Aziru and his troops had gained control of it. Aziru also controlled the lines of communication so messengers from the palace are unable to get to Rib-Hadda. In a desperate measure Rib-Hadda had tried to smuggle some of his men into Sumur. But that backfired; the ever-alert Yappah Hadda once again had them captured and bound. Rib-Hadda then asks the king to send a royal commissioner to decide who is right.

EA 117   *Rib-Hadda's scribe sat at the table with his stylus positioned over his wet clay tablet ready to take the dictation and had sent another letter to the indifferent pharaoh. Even now the scribe was beginning to question his lord's inflexible loyalty to a man who clearly didn't give a damn about him. As the situation deteriorated, forbidden thoughts started to enter the scribe's mind; perhaps it was time to defect to Aziru rather than be killed in the inevitable onslaught, and then Rib-Hadda interrupted the scribe's reverie and spoke "Say to the great King..." and the scribe began to write the message.*

In previous messages the Pharaoh had asked Rib-Hadda the rhetorical question of why he continues to write so frequently. Of course, anybody else on the planet, would have taken the hint and quit writing. However, since Rib-Hadda is the conductor of the 'one note symphony' he is oblivious to the hint and states that he, alone, among all of the mayors is the most loyal to the king and as such wants his majesty to know what the situation in the Levant is like.

Finally, Rib-Hadda complains that the two men that he has sent to the palace are apparently still being detained for unknown reasons.

This letter appears to be written to either Smenkhare or Tutankhamen since he reminds the king that that Akhenaten had sent Ammanapa out with a small force against Abdi-Asirta. As result they had captured him and taken everything he had stolen, so why shouldn't the present king do the same?

Rib-Hadda says that the entire area is aligned with the Apiru. He then beseeches the king to write to Yanhamu and Pihura.

And then once again Rib-Hadda returns to the theme that he still has litigation against Yappah Hadda and Ha-ip. To entice the king to act he says that everything in the decision will be awarded to the king.

EA 118   The war against Rib-Hadda is severe. But even in the middle of the war he again reminds the king that he has litigation pending and asks that a commissioner be sent to hear his case. Rib-Hadda tells after a settlement is reached the king can take anything he wants for himself, or he can give it to the mayors.

Rib-Hadda complains, that as usual, there are no provisions for the peasantry and now they have gone off to the sons of Abdi-Asirta. He complains that if the remaining peasantry leaves, the city will fall to the Apiru.

The war is against him and Yanhamu now and he says that Yanhamu is a loyal servant.

EA 119 Rib-Hadda complains that there are people slandering him saying that he was responsible for the death of the king's archers. Rib-Hadda tells the king that since all of the commissioners are alive (seeing how they have a high mortality rate this seems notable) and that he should consult with them to find out what the truth is. He notes that there will be a second tablet outlining everything that Yappah Hadda has stolen from him.

EA 120   In some ways this is one of the most pertinent, albeit fragmentary letters in the corpus. It's very easy to overlook, or ignore, since it's merely an inventory of things that were allegedly stolen by Yappah-hada. And unsurprisingly Rib-Hadda either wants everything back or else he wants compensation for his loss. The inventory list goes from the utterly mundane, noting that one hammer was stolen, to much more luxurious items such as a bed that was overlaid with gold, along with a chair that was also overlaid with gold.

The next items in the inventory are deadly! Rib-Hadda claims that100 swords and 100 daggers were also stolen. So apparently Yappah-Hadda also raided Rib-Hadda's armory! Not only that but he blasted his way into Rib-Hadda's treasury and stole100 shekels of gold. And finally, the most amazing thing was that he kidnapped 90 to 100 maidservants!

This was obviously a meticulously planned raid by Yappah-Hadda who undoubtedly had horses, carts, and various other accoutrements to make sure that it was a success. Of course, there's always the possibility that this was the result of a series of raids by Yappah-Hadda but the tone of the letter suggests that it was probably a single raid that yielded all of this booty.

The critical thing is that we know after reading this list of stolen goods that it is transparently obvious why the king was reluctant to send anything to Rib-Hadda. After all he knew there was a good chance that the man would lose everything to Yappah-Hadda, Zimredda, or Aziru.

Then in the closing section there is mention that the king sent Abdi-Hadda and Ben-aZimi (sic) to evidently retrieve a woman, whose name has been lost.

Evidently this list is the second tablet mentioned in EA 119 that had been sent to the king so that he could render a judgement either for or against Yappah-Hadda. Unfortunately, as usual we don't know how this case was resolved.

EA 121 This is another letter that follows the usual monotonous point-counterpoint format in which Rib-Hadda asks for archers, the King, as usual, doesn't send any archers and then Rib-Hadda complaining about the fact that he hasn't received any archers.

These protestations become so regular and tedious that it's like watching an already boring ping-pong match being played in slow motion.

EA 122   In this letter Rib-Hadda accuses Pahurra of committing 'an enormity' when he sent troops on a raid to kill the Sirdanu people, and then kidnapped 3 others and sent them to Egypt. Rib-Hadda asks that the men be returned to him.

EA 123   *Rib Hadda read the latest tablet from one of his correspondents. Pahurra had sent troops into land of Sirdanu on a raid. After killing numerous innocent civilians, he had captured three of the highest-ranking members of the Sirdanu society, and then for reasons of his own, sent them off to Akhet-Aten where they would be safe from anybody trying to make a rescue mission to recover them.*

Pihurra has sent troops to kill the Sirdanu people and during the raid kidnapped 3 people sending them to Akhet-Aten. Apparently, these were three high ranking people because Rib-Hadda is demanding that they be returned to him lest the people revolt against him. Then he names the men Abdi-Rama, Yattin-Hadda, Abdi-Milki

EA 124   The city of Gubla alone remains to Rib-Hadda. Aziru tightening his grip on the Levant by boasting that the cities of Rib-Hadda have been taken. Rib-Hadda once again wonders why the king stands idly by while Aziru continues to kill the mayors who refuse to join. From this letter it is clear that assassinating his opponents is Aziru's favorite method of gaining power, while ignoring these murders is Akhenaten's response.

As a result of the murders of Abdi-Asirta and Pawura, Rib-Hadda says that Aziru claims that the pharaoh will no longer come out to the Levant. Rib-Hadda is obliquely stating that since the pharaoh has abandoned the Levant it will be easier for Aziru to take complete control of it.

Rib-Hadda then says that there are no oxen, goats, or sheep. And once again repeats his request that the Pharaoh send out archers and charioteers to retake the cities that he has lost, otherwise the King will never recover them.

EA 125   *Aziru and his brothers had launched a raid on the city in the middle of the night. Aided by the Apiru they had stolen all of his oxen, sheep, and goats. The peasants, who could clearly see the handwriting on the wall, decided that it was time to leave. So unsurprisingly they left both in broad daylight or the middle of the night abandoning Rib-Hadda to his fate.*

This clearly is a reply to a letter that the king had sent Rib-Hadda, because as usual, the King predictably tells him to 'guard the city'. And Rib-Hadda, as always, rebuts the king with his snarky "What am I going to use to defend the city?" After that Rib-Hadda complains that in previous years he had received grain and supplies but now he is getting nothing.

By now Aziru has repeatedly raided Rib-Hadda's countryside stolen all of his oxen and goats and sheep. As a result, the peasants who are getting tired of this endless war are abandoning the city and going elsewhere for food.

Evidently, in the king's now lost letter to Rib-Hadda, the king had evidently compared Rib-Hadda to other mayors, and unsurprisingly, found him coming up short.

Rib-Hadda says that the peasantry is abandoning him. He then explains that the reason the other mayors have their peasants under control is because Aziru isn't attacking them. But the price that Rib-Hadda is paying for defying Aziru, is that Aziru has control of Rib-Hadda's cities and is choking off his food supply.

It is obvious that the King wrote and tried to get Rib-Hadda to settle the problems peacefully to which Rib-Hadda says how can he make peace with Aziru when he is trying to kill Rib-Hadda and take over his cities?

He closes with his usual accusation that the dogs of Abdi-Asirta do as they please and set fires to the cities of the king.

EA 126   *Rib-Hadda read the letter from the Pharaoh. Rib-Hadda had hoped that the Pharaoh would be sending troops and chariots to finally drive Aziru from the land and finally, restore the Levant to his majesty the king. However, it contained nothing. It was merely an order for him to deliver a shipment of 'boxwood' as soon as possible.*

This letter is obviously a reply to a letter from the pharaoh, in which he ordered boxwood from the land of Salhi and also from Ugarit. The problem is that since the sons of Abdi-Asirta are at war with Rib-Hadda he can't send his ships there to fulfill the order.

Rib-Hadda then complains that all the rest of the mayors, (who are clearly better diplomats than he is since they are all at peace with the sons of Abdi-Asirta) can send their ships anywhere they want.

This of course leads to Rib-Hadda complaining that while the other mayors are evidently receiving plenty of supplies from the palace; Rib-Hadda, as usual, isn't getting a thing. He then plaintively asks why is he being ignored? He wonders why the king is abandoning the city. And if that's the case then why he doesn't replace Rib-Hadda's with someone else if he isn't satisfied with his performance?

Which frankly is a question I've been thinking about for a long time, however if the king answered him, it has been lost to history.

Next Rib-Hadda says that he keeps sending messengers to the king but for some reason they never return. Given this amazing attrition rate I can't help but wonder whether once the messengers arrived in Akhet-Aten and saw all that the city had to offer that they just decided to stay there. After all life is short and why not stay in beautiful Akhet-Aten rather than return to certain short, nasty brutish world that was in Gubla?

Finally, on the international front Rib-Hadda mentions that Hittite troops have set fire to the countryside and that they are mobilizing their troops to seize Gubla. Evidently Suppiluliumas is beginning his assault in the Northern Levant. We already know this will end when Suppiluliumas conquers the area. And we also know that once that happens Abdi-Asirta and his micro-kingdom will be absorbed into the Hittite empire and vanish forever from history.

EA 127   *The war against Rib-Hadda was severe. Self-doubt, the poison that could defeat armies, was beginning to spread through the ranks of his men and they were becoming more rebellious and reluctant to fight as Rib-Hadda could neither win a decisive battle against his enemies nor negotiate a meaningful peace with Aziru.*

In this letter Rib-Hadda makes his usual appeal to the pharaoh to send more troops to evacuate him and unsurprisingly there's no evidence that the King pays any attention to him. Rib-Hadda airs his complaint that everyone is against him and appeals to the Pharaoh to speak to Yanhamu, one of the Pharaoh's commissioners, to advise him of what the situation is really like. At this point in time, I'm beginning to wonder what, if anything, Yanhamu is telling the pharaoh. Clearly, the evidence leans lopsidedly to the fact the king either isn't listening to Yanhamu, or Yanhamu is telling the king to disregard Rib-Hadda's complaints.

Finally, Rib-Hadda says that if Gubla is joined to the Apiru then there will be no way that they can get troops from Egypt into the city.

Rib-Hadda complains that in previous years when Abdi Asirta had come up against him, Rib-Hadda, was strong, but now there is dissention within the troops and he is hard pressed to control them. Rib-Hadda closes by asking for 200 soldiers and 30 chariots, to guard the city.

EA 128   Message lost.

EA 129   *Rib-Hadda continued thinking about the problems that surrounded him. As usual Aziru continued to attack the various cities in the Levant. It was a brutal fact that but commissioners came and*

The sons of Abdi-Asirta are now continuing the war against Rib-Hadda that their father had started. Among other things they have killed an Egyptian commissioner. And after getting away with that murder they have taken all of the cities except Batruna and of course, they intend to take Gubla.

Rib-Hadda is baffled. He says that the king has written to him and told him that archers were coming to his rescue, but so far, they haven't arrived. Rib-Hadda ominously predicts that if the archers don't come out this year, then the city will fall. In closing a desperate Rib-Hadda says that if the king isn't going to send archers, then send ships so he can be safely evacuated and return to Egypt.

At this point, there is a break in the tablet, so we don't know what was written. After the break, Rib-Hadda mentions that the Hittites are active in the area but doesn't give any details. It's obvious that the Hittites are muscling their way into the Levant, and that Aziru was probably forming some kind of an alliance with them in order to take control of some of the outlying cities.

Finally, they took Sumur and killed Pewuru the commissioner of the king.

EA 130 *Rib-Hadda read the letter the king had sent him. A new commissioner named Irrimayasa had been sent to the region. But so far, the man hadn't arrived. The king has predictably ordered Rib-Hadda to guard the city. Rib-Hadda is baffled. After all, hasn't the king read his many previous letters where he said he had no troops to guard the city?*

This is another typical letter that is clearly a reply to a letter from the king, who as usual orders Rib-Hadda to 'guard the city'. Rib-Hadda then replies with his usual shopping list of excuses as to why he can't do it.

He starts with the fact that the king supposedly sent a man named Irimayassa to Rib-Hadda. Rib-Hadda complains that the man hasn't arrived. Of course, the fact that he hasn't arrived might be for numerous reasons. However, we can be fairly certain that the man did arrive and the reason for this is, because long after Rib-Hadda is dead, we find Irimayassa being dispatched by the king in EA 370 to resolve a conflict with the ruler of Asqaluna.

Unsurprisingly, Rib-Hadda makes the usual complaints that in previous times the Pharaoh had sent a garrison to help defend Rib-Hadda but now there are no troops being sent which leads to his usual rhetorical question of "how am I supposed to defend myself"?

Rib-Hadda predictably complains that the other mayors are busy attacking him while he alone is loyal to the pharaoh. And then he finally closes with the usual sullen warning that he will guard the city but who will guard it when he is dead?

EA 131   *Aziru looked out at the city of Sumur. His troops had now surrounded the city, and were simply waiting for the order to attack. And then it was given, they fell on the city and killed the garrison that was defending it. In the next couple of weeks, he regrouped and began his attack on Gubla.*

Meanwhile Pewuru the commissioner had been sent to the Northern Levant to administer the affairs of the king. It didn't take long before Aziru discovered the commissioner's location, and quickly dispatched his assassins.

Pewuru looked up at the men as they burst into his residence carrying swords and axes, their faces hidden behind the masks that they wore. He turned to look for an escape; there was none. Within a second, they had closed in on him; he raised one hand in a futile effort to block the blow and then watched as it was sliced off by the axe wielding Apiru. His hand fell to the floor like a branch that had been snipped. Pewuru was in shock for a second as he looked in dismay at the bloody stump spurting blood like a fountain and then gazed, at his upturned hand laying uselessly on the floor. But it was just a second, before another one of the men slammed the spear into his stomach, Pewuru felt a brief agonizing explosion of excruciating pain as the spear ripped through his guts. He glanced down and watched as his bowels came slithering out of his abdomen like a large snake emerging from its winter hiding place. Then just before he died, he pondered the absurdity of it all, he had been sent to guard the Lands of the King and now he was dying as a result of his loyalty. And then the chasm of death opened and he fell headfirst into it.

Then they dragged his body out in the street where it was left to rot.

Tragically, another commissioner has been killed. And Rib-Hadda makes the usual claim that Sumur has been seized and that the troops of Gubla have been killed. Amazingly after this apparent disaster Rib-Hadda then makes a request for 300 soldiers, along with 30 chariots, and 100 men from Kasi to guard the city. Rib-Hadda writes that he is worried that his troops will desert him. Assuming that the previous military disasters did in fact happen then this is something well worth worrying about.

However just when you thought things couldn't get worse, they got worse. Evidently the king's counselor Pewuru was murdered and his body thrown in the street with no funeral offerings and left there to rot.

Rib-Hadda also notes that Panhamnata wouldn't listen to him and as a result he continues with his treacherous activities. Then after Panhamnata dies his son took over the reins of government and continue the family tradition continued of undermining Rib-Hadda.

He closes by telling the king to ask Yanhamu about the activities that are going on in Rib-Hadda's domain.

EA 132   *Rib Hadda thought about the past. He called his scribe; the man took out one of his moist clay tablets and prepared to write. Say to the king my lord message of Rib-Hadda…*

This letter was probably written to either Smenkhare or Tutankhamen since Rib-Hadda refers to a previous letter where he had written *"earlier I wrote to your father"*. With this little historical tidbit, we can begin to narrow down to which king Rib-Hadda was addressing.

At this point in time, we know there are only three royal males and possibly two women that we know of who were either pharaoh, or in line to be pharaoh when the letters were written. The three were Akhenaten, Smenkhare, and Tutankhamen.

The two women were Nefertiti, Akhenaten's wife Nefertiti. And a younger daughter who was also named Nefertiti.

In this letter for the first time, we see a specific change in the leadership; the king is dead, long live the king. Akhenaten has left the building.

And so, we have finally arrived at the well-known succession issue. This is topic that I have effortlessly managed to dodge up until now. It is a subject, (that like the alleged co-regency issue) much ink has been spilled, but little of consequence has been written. So, who exactly succeeded Akhenaten? Was it his wife Nefertiti? His daughter also named Nefertiti? Or was it Smenkhare? Tutankhamen is eliminated because we know for a fact that he followed Smenkhare.

Of course, this leads back to our initial question of who was Rib-Hadda's letter addressed to then?

To answer that question, we have to take a detour into the Valley of the Kings and from there to an obscure tomb known simply as KV 55. It is here that we find one of the most enduring mysteries of Amarna. In the 19th century excavators discovered a tiny reinternment of a member of the royal family. Since the body was found in a woman's sarcophagus at first it was, naturally, thought to be a female. Subsequent investigation proved that it was actually a male. Unfortunately, the original name on the coffin had been chiseled out, and infuriatingly no new name hadn't been inserted. As a result of this we don't know who it was originally designed for nor do we know who was reinterred in it.

Fortunately, there were other clues.

The canopic chest was clearly for Kiya one of Akhenaten's subsidiary wives, and a partial funeral shrine that had been made for Queen Tiye was found abandoned. And finally, there were 'magic bricks' made out of Nile mud that had one of Akhenaten's earlier names written on it. With these facts we can begin a process of elimination. As I said earlier there were only three royal males that we know of at the time. Akhenaten, Tutankhamen, and Smenkhare. Tutankhamen can be eliminated because his tomb and body had already been discovered. We know for a fact that Smenkhare died before Tut since his solid gold funeral mask was recycled for Tut's funeral. That leaves Smenkhare and Akhenaten as potential candidates. However, Rib-Hadda specifically says 'your father' therefore we can conclude that he was talking about the present king's biological father and not an honorific title.

Well, these days we can resolve the problem with DNA. Studies have shown that the mummy in KV 55 is indeed the father of Tutankhamen. In addition to that the 'magic bricks' with Akhenaten's earlier throne name seals it in my opinion (see Reeves).

Alright but what about the possibility that Rib-Hadda was actually writing to one of the two Nefertiti's? That's a great question and it deserves a great answer and unfortunately, I don't have it. The evidence seems to suggest that it was either Smenkhare or Tutankhamen.

In this letter Rib-Hadda makes reference to a previous time when Abdi-Asirta had attacked him. At that time Rib Hadda had written to the palace and as a result Akhenaten had sent archers out to Ammuru and subsequently captured Abdi-Asirta. Abdi Asirta was evidently released and returned to the Levant because we know that he was murdered in EA 101.

He then tells the king to consult with Yanhamu about the time Rib-Hadda advised Yanhamu not to make an alliance with Abdi-Asirta and that if he had then Abdi-Asirta would make him a prisoner. Yanhamu (according to Rib-Hadda) wisely did as he was told, guarded the king's cities and survived as a result.

Rib-Hadda also gave the same advice to Pawuru to ignore Ha'ip's entreaties. But of course, Pawuru ignored Rib-Hadda and now Ha'ip is in control of Sumur, and finally a commissioner had been killed.

Pihura will not be satisfied with his conquests so far and instead he will kill the rest of the mayors. Rib-Hadda wants ships to help him leave, and almost 200 men along with chariots and archers for his defense.

EA 362   *Rib Hadda called his scribe in to begin taking dictation of his latest message to the King. The war against Gubla was severe Abdi-Asirta's sons and the Apiru had surrounded the city and it would probably fall before long. But that wasn't the only problem. This was another traitorous mayor that had spread the word that there was a pandemic in the country and that everybody was sick. Once again it was just another lie in an endless series of lies that needed to be squelched.*

Rib Hadda finally spoke. "Say to the King my lord."

This letter which is numbered EA 362 is clearly out of order from the main sequences of Rib-Hadda's letters the problem becomes exactly where does it belong? Obviously, it should be in a much earlier part of the chronology when Rib-Hadda is making various requests for archers. As far as I can tell this is the only letter where he says his request has actually been granted.

This is one of the few letter that gives tactical information in it. In this case Rib-Hadda says that if defends Gubla by moves to the outlying areas then his men will desert him.

Based on the slim internal evidence, this letter clearly belongs somewhere after EA 101 after Abdi-Asirta is murdered. Unfortunately, there isn't enough evidence to determine exactly where it belongs since our only clue is the fact that it references the sons of Abdi-Asirta attacking him it clearly takes place after Abdi-Asirta's death.

Rib-Hadda asks the king to send more archers to Gubla and if he doesn't then Gubla will fall and they all will die. Once again, we get these recurring references to 'plagues' or 'pestilences' being endemic in the middle east, but alas they don't specify what the symptoms are or how many have died. In this case Rib-Hadda denies that there is pestilence in the land and says that in fact ended a long time ago.

Finally in a telling sentence many mayors are against archers coming out, Rib-Hadda says since they're at peace and don't want to disturb the status quo.

And finally, Rib-Hadda notes that they've killed the commissioner Pewure.

EA 133   In this short epistle the sons of Abdi-Asirta have apparently taken control of all the cities. This time Rib-Hadda wants only ten men sent from Meluhha.

At this point in time, I have to admit I'm completely baffled as to what Rib-Hadda thought he could do with ten men. Especially in view of the fact that in previous letters he had asked for 400 men along with 30 chariots! Frankly, I find it difficult to believe that the pharaoh wasn't also similarly baffled. And unsurprisingly there's no indication that he granted the request for this platoon size group of men.

Was this an act of desperation on Rib-Hadda's part to get any kind of military aid? Or is this letter simply out of place and it actually belongs at an earlier place before Abdi-Asirta had gathered all of his strength?

Unfortunately, there isn't enough evidence to make a decision one way or the other on this question.

E.A 134 *Rib-Hadda listened to the priests as they gave him the bad news; all of their prayers had gone unanswered. The offerings they had made to the gods had been refused. And finally, there were no signs indicating what course of action should be taken to forestall the invasion that Aziru was planning. The short and tragic message was that the gods had abandoned the people. They were on their own now.*

In this letter Rib-Hadda say the war being waged by Aziru is growing severe. How severe? Well now Rib-Hadda claims that even the gods have abandoned Gubla and that Aziru is preparing to attack the city. The people have deserted Rib-Hadda and are now looking for provisions elsewhere.

In the never-ending toxic relationship between the palace and Rib-Hadda he complains that he has sent a man to the palace and as usual the king hasn't written back.

EA 135 message lost.

EA 136 *Rib-Hadda was exhausted, both physically and emotionally. His own wife and men had urged him to make peace with Abdi-asirti. But he had refused. Instead, he had ridden to another mayor named Ammunira in order to make peace with him. And unsurprisingly he had failed, and now that he returned home, he found that his younger brother had barred him from entering his house.*

Again, in this short epistle we get an intimate portrait of the interfamilial strife that is going on within Rib-Hadda's own family. In this case his own wife and brother can clearly see the handwriting on the wall, that the sons of Abdi-Asirta are closing in and it's time to shift alliances. But Rib-Hadda as mule-headed as ever refuses to listen to them, and instead pursues a fool's errand of trying to make an alliance with Ammunira. Of course, this ham-handed attempt at diplomacy fails and Rib-Hadda returns home only to find that he has been barred from entry into his home by his own brother.

But the ruthless brutality of Rib-Hadda's brother is revealed in the closing sentence when he says that two of Rib-Hadda's wives and two of his own sons have been given over to the rebels undoubtedly as hostages in order to forestall an invasion.

EA 137 *Rib-Hadda watched as his man returned from Akhet-Aten. The man dismounted from his horse and gave Rib-Hadda the bad news; the pharaoh had nothing to say to Rib-Hadda, there were no messages, there were no supplies, there was simply… nothing.*

But as usual Rib-Hadda was undeterred. He began dictating another letter to the Pharaoh, who as usual continued to turn a deaf hear to his most faithful servant.

Rib-Hadda, now broke, goes to Hammuniri to seek some aid. And while he is there his treacherous younger brother turns against him and unites Gubla against Rib-Hadda. When Rib-Hadda returned empty handed, (foreshadowing Shakespeare and King Lear) Rib-Hadda is driven from the city. Rib-Hadda then says that he cannot enter Egypt because he is old and sick. Instead, he sends his son to make the usual request for troops to stop the sons of Abdi-asirti from taking control

Rib-Hadda then makes his usual attempt to appeal to the king's greed by saying there is plenty of gold and silver in the city and if the pharaoh wants it's his for the taking.

In these final highly autobiographical letters, we get an intense and personal insight into the agony of Rib-Hadda's plight. In these last months and days, we watch as his life slips away from him like sand in an hour glass. The end of his life foreshadows Greek tragedy where the hero has great qualities, and even greater flaws that cause his downfall and death. He is a bronze age version of Shakespeare's, destitute, and homeless King Lear being driven from one city to another by his treacherous family. Only in this case it isn't a play but a real live breathing person who is now coming to the end of his life and giving us an unvarnished, and pitiless review of his circumstances.

Rib-Hadda's messenger has returned empty handed, with no money, no weapons, and no soldiers.

When he had gone to Hammuniri, Rib-Hadda's younger brother stirred up trouble in the city of Gubla and had driven him from the city.

Apparently in a letter that the Pharaoh had written to Rib-Hadda he had told him to return to Egypt, but Rib-Hadda defers saying that he is old and sick and won't be able to make it to the palace. Instead, he sends his son in his place.

Rib-Hadda says that the gods of Gubla are harsh and they are punishing him for the mistakes he has made in the past.

He makes another request that more archers be sent to the city and claims that there are plenty of people who are still loyal the crown, and that he can retake the city with ease.

Rib-Hadda then tries to make a ham-handed bribe to the king telling him that the temples have much gold and silver in them and that it will be his for the taking if he so desires.

He closes the letter begging the king to take it over and restore it to his control.

EA 138   Rib-Hadda was exhausted, but that changed nothing; life continued on in its blood splattered trajectory no matter what happened. There was now a new king in Akhet-Aten since the old king had 'spread his wings and flown to the west' which was the Egyptian euphemism for death.

Rib-Hadda decided that it was time to write a letter that would give a brief overview of his plight and how he needed the Pharaoh's help now more than ever.

Apparently, this is a letter to a different king and from the tone of the letter Akhenaten has evidently died. In our culture we would expect an extensive correspondence on the death of a monarch. But from what I can see the death of a monarch in ancient history is either ignored or just a quick note that they had died; there's never any condolences in them. Deaths are always treated rather indifferently and without much fanfare in the letters. As such any letters from Akhet-Aten to Rib-Hadda informing him of the king's demise have either been lost or, far less likely, were never written in the first place.

That as we know by now was the hallmark of Akhenaten's foreign policy, either do nothing, or as little as possible. The importance of this conjecture about Akhenaten's death is that it gives us a fairly strong relative time line concerning Rib-Hadda's time in office. We know that Akhenaten ruled for about fifteen years, and that there were two ephemeral rulers after his death who probably ruled for no more than two years before Tut came to power. They were Smenkhare and "Nefertiti". However, since Rib-Hadda says "King" we can probably rule out "Nefertiti" as a recipient and safely say that it was Smenkhare who received the letter. Since he ruled for a maximum of two years before his death, then this would fit in with the three to fourth month cycle of letters that Rib-Hadda would send to the palace. If this conjecture is correct then it probably means that Rib-Hadda died in Smenkhare's reign.

In this letter things have decidedly taken a turn for the worse for Rib-Hadda; a year earlier there had been a revolt in Gubla which had forced Rib-Hadda into exile in Beirut which is where this letter originated.

Rib-Hadda then recounts how when Abdi-asrati seized Sumur it was Rib-Hadda who had single handedly defended it. Eventually troops came out and took Abdi-asirti and was subsequently released.

The people grew tired of the constant battles with Abdi-Asirta and revolted. Rib-Hadda instantly crushed the rebellion and killed the rebels. Then amazingly the people made the rather pertinent point of asking where Rib-Hadda was going to get people to run the city if he killed everybody? This rather compelling argument resonates with Rib-Hadda who apparently breaks off the slaughter and sends another letter to the palace requesting troops, and of course none are sent.

But even though there was now a nominal peace, the people still wanted to join Abdi-asrati however Rib-Hadda refused and they started to rebel. This time his brother stepped in and apparently quelled the revolt peacefully. This allowed Rib-Hadda to go to Hammuniri for discussions about reinforcements. These negotiations generated nothing, and when Rib-Hadda returns, he finds the city is now under Aziru's control.

What happened?

Evidently, once Rib-Hadda had left, Aziru planted rumors that Rib-Hadda was either dead or no longer in control of the city, and consequently the city no longer owed any allegiance to Rib-Hadda. Rib-Hadda of course vigorously disagreed with this assessment and drove the troops of Aziru from the city and took over the city.

But even though Rib-Hadda was nominally in control of the city his grip on the situation was tenuous; after all half of the city was still sympathetic to Aziru, and ready to overthrow Rib-Hadda the moment the opportunity presented itself. So, in order to solidify his position Rib-Hadda sends his son to Akhet-Aten to request more troops. And then, with utter predictability, once his son reaches the palace he is immediately 'detained' for four months with no explanation as to why this is happening. But even though Rib-Hadda pleads for more troops arguing that he could easily drive Abdi-Asirta out and retake the city for the king and restore it to its former glory he receives none.

Rib-Hadda then tells how Abdi -Asirta (evidently in a reference to a past raid) took the treasures of the city and gave them to Aziru. Unsurprisingly there are factions within Beirut that apparently want Aziru driven out, but he evidently controls the grain supply and as a result controls the city.

Rib-Hadda then goes on to say that he doesn't know how long he can stay with Hamminuri and is concerned with Aziru invading Beirut.

Finally, the letter closes with the prophetic and ominous warning that once Rib-Hadda is dead his sons will inherit the same murderous mess that he has been dealing with for years. In the end they too will continue writing to the palace for relief, from whomever is oppressing them.

And with that the final letter draws to a sinister conclusion.

Rib-Hadda laid down for the last time that night to sleep. He was exhausted and now as he approached his fortieth birthday, he was an old man. He knew that the next day would contain another set of problems with Aziru and his murderous clan. And then Rib-Hadda finally drifted off to sleep. He didn't hear the barefoot steps of the assassin who had slipped into is room that night, nor did he feel the knife plunging into his neck. Rib-Hadda's body jerked spasmodically. The assassin pulled the knife out and shoved it in another part of Rib-Hadda's throat. He watched Rib-Hadda's body move convulsively and a moment later it stopped moving and went limp. The assassin listened carefully for any approaching footsteps and hearing none, he slipped out into the night undetected.

The next morning Rib-Hadda's body was discovered. Funeral arrangements were hastily made and Rib-Hadda was buried without fanfare or ceremony. His brother was installed as Mayor, who then sent off an obligatory tablet to the Pharaoh that Rib-Hadda was dead, and now he merely waited for his lord and master to instruct him on what to do next.

The next day the new Mayor of Gubla called the scribe in and began to dictate "Say to the King my lord message of Ili-rapih. Here are the crimes of Aziru…"

Chapter 12

Gotterdammerung-The Twilight of the Gods

Götterdämmerung- "Twilight of the Gods" is of course a reference to the Icelandic and Nordic myth describing how the princess Brunhilda who after a lover's battle (and in keeping with Shakespeare's famous dictum "that hell hath no fury like a woman scorned"), proceeds to set fire to Valhalla and burns it to the ground.

The German composer, and notorious anti-Semite Richard Wagner, then transformed this myth into an opera known as "The Ring Cycle". A few decades later, a wannabe artist by the name of Adolph Hitler, who was obsessed with Wagner's music, (and who was even a more notorious antisemite than Wagner could ever possibly hope to be)-, set Wagner's music to action and proceeded to burn down most of Europe, invaded Russia, and practically wiped out the +Jewish population in the process.

Fortunately, J.R.R. Tolkien took the myth ran it through his typewriter and it morphed into what would eventually become the multi-bazillion dollar "The Lord of the Rings" franchise. Moral of the story? Anybody who thinks that myths don't have power should reconsider their position.

Alas, we poor Amarnaphiles are still waiting for our Tolkien to arrive.

Something similar to this happened at the city of Akhet-Aten. Only instead of Brunhilda destroying Valhalla, it was probably General Horemhab, who was the last Pharaoh of the 18th dynasty who destroyed Akhet-Aten and razed it to the ground. But in the time-honored tradition of 'waste not, want not' he then recycled the blocks in his various construction projects. They were subsequently recovered in modern times and we now have a fairly good idea of what some of the buildings looked like.

After that Akhet-Aten was deserted until it was rediscovered in the 19th century, and its history has slowly been recovered.

Aristotle in his book the Poetics said that every tragedy has three parts, a beginning, middle, and end. This structure is what is known as 'The Three Act Play'. Though I should quickly say that this rule also applies to virtually everything; there is a beginning, middle and end to it. And the same principle applies here to historical accounts.

I'm sure if you're like me you wonder how the story ends. To start with what happens after Rib-Hadda, and Abdi-Asirta die? Well, we know that after Abdi-Asirta died his son Aziru took over and continued his father's time-honored strategy of killing various mayors, commissioners and absorbing their cities into his micro-kingdom. And we also know that he relied on the Apiru to help him in this enterprise. In addition to that we know he successfully broke away from the Egyptian empire for a brief period of time, until the great white shark of the middle east, known as the Hittite empire, swallowed him like the insignificant sardine that he was.

In order to find out the rest of Aziru's story we have to first turn away from the Amarna letters and search the Hittite peace treaties to find out what happened next. And it's here that we discover the continuation of our tale. In the treaty Suppiluliumas Says that Aziru 'approached' (i.e., more than likely Aziru faced the music that Suppiluliumas would wipe him from the face of the earth, like the traitorous dog that he was, if he didn't accede to Supp's. demands.) the Hittites and asked to be accepted as a vassal.

Interestingly part of the treaty says that he is to pay one hundred shekels of gold per year as tribute to Suppiluliumas How much is that? Well 300 shekels of gold is about 3,134 grams of gold is worth almost 200,000 dollars in today's market.   By today's standards of oligarchs, and millionaires, billionaires and trillionaires, that is an insignificant sum. Once Aziru is absorbed into the Hittite empire he vanishes from the historical record without a trace.

Next what happened to the feared Apiru? Well, they also disappear into the historical void without a trace of what happened to them.

Akhenaten of course died and was buried in his tomb in Akhet-Aten. After his death two ephemeral rulers took over and also vanished into history. Then the world-famous boy King Tutankhamen took over and moved the capital back to Thebes. After he died his uncle Ay ruled briefly before going to rest in his 'house of eternity'. With his passing the powerful General Horemhab took control, and since he had no children, he appointed his successor. When Horemhab died, the 18th dynasty drew to a close and that is where we'll end our story.

Conclusion

The frustration with the Amarna letters is that they conceal as much as they reveal. In this case we get a lopsided, in-depth insight into the murderous activities of the mayors in particular and maybe a couple of dozen of their subordinates in the Levant in general, and about events that took place during an extremely narrow time frame. The letters themselves all deal with an extraordinarily limited number of subjects; mainly intrigues, wars and conspiracies going on between the various participants.

The lack of dating of the correspondence also leaves us with questions. With the exception of one or two letters, no correspondence is dated. Therefore, we have no timeframe for the series of letters or the time between responses. Well, the one thing that I discovered that can give us a clue, is the fact that Rib-Hadda would occasionally say that it had been three to four months since he had sent his last letter. This gave me a tentative time frame for the journey time of a letter. It would take about a month and a half to two months for a letter to make the trip to Akhet-Aten, and the same amount of time to make it back to Rib-Hadda. Three months maximum. If it went to four months Rib-Hadda would fire off another tablet 'reminding' the king that he hadn't answered the first letter.

Rib-Hadda wrote about 70 letters that have been preserved. In several of his letters, as I noted earlier, he says it has been three to four months since he sent his last letter. Well doing the math, if Rib-Hadda sent a letter every three to four months that means the correspondence took place over a minimum of 17.5 years to a maximum of 23.3 years. From the internal evidence we know he was in power while Amenhotep III was alive and survived into at least Smenkhare and possibly Tutankamen's reign. As such this relative time frame falls well within the accepted chronology of the Amarna kings and we can reasonably say that was the length of Rib-Hadda's career.

Unfortunately, with the exception of a few letters from various anonymous women we know nothing about what the opposite sex was doing while these intrigues were swirling around them. It's small foundation on which to build a large pyramid.

So, all things considered we have an excellent, highly gender-biased assessment, of the situation in Rib-Hadda's epistles. How accurate is it? From what I can see nothing in the other Amarna letters, or the historical records flat out contradicts anything Rib-Hada was saying or writing about. And the fact that nothing much changed after his death merely reasserts the basic premise that the Northern Levant was a constant battle between the various combatants in this area. In the end these tin horn war lords, mini-monarchs, and wannabe emperors rose and fell like the tides of the sea, only to be replaced by others after they either died of natural causes or more likely were murdered.

In the meantime, empires came and went but the perennially shifting borders of the middle east along with the bloody confrontations that have gone on from that day to this are the only constant in middle-eastern politics.

So, what can we conclude from our study of Rib-Hadda? What kind of assessment can we make of the man and his times? Naturally I'm overflowing with thoughts and comments about it. And the first one that comes to mind is that he was without doubt the most vociferous of the mayors. Even though the other mayors were evidently suffering the same or similar problems, Rib-Hadda was the only one who wrote constantly, about how he was suffering at the hands of the Apiru and Abdi-Asirta. However, I hasten to add that this observation is hardly a novel observation, and every Amarnologist from the pharaoh's ministers to me have noted how Rib-Hadda is the loudest and most demanding of all of the Amarna characters.

On a different note, though I have to confess that reading Rib-Hadda can be a struggle. After all, how many times can he throw himself at the feet of the king 7 times and 7 times, before you wonder why he hasn't crushed his ribs into talcum powder? In addition to that one wonders what things looked like on the ground? For instance, Rib-Hadda keeps stating over and over that Sumer has fallen, but was it the same time or a different time or is it just a reminder to the king that the situation is dire? And finally, after a while you get tired of working your way through the accusations of the high crimes and misdemeanors of Abdi-Asirta and wish that Rib-Hadda would just once spell them out in detail.

Fortunately, after plodding through one tiresome accusation after another, and reading about the treasonous activities of Abdi-Asirta you finally get to the one gem that you've been waiting for; that Abdi-Asirta has finally been killed. And now, at last, you are grateful that you'll never have to hear about Abdi-Asirta again. Except that it just gets worse after his sons take over under the stewardship of his son Aziru.

Another thing that I began to wonder about was why didn't the Pharaoh replace Rib-Hadda with a more dynamic and assertive mayor? Surely there had to be a mayor that would put a stop to Abdi-Asirta's treacherous behavior once and for all. In this case I think after you have read the entire corpus of the Amarna letters the answer slowly comes into focus. Why? Well, in virtually all of the letters we see other mayors were attacking and being attacked by yet other mayors. In fact, it seemed to be the number one spectator sport of the mid-east. And yet the king did nothing about it. Then as we extend our historical inquiries outwards, we find that these revolts weren't just confined to the Egyptians. In the Mittanian empire the various provinces were also rebelling against their overlords the most notable group were the Assyrians. Meanwhile in the north Hatti's various provinces and people there were also seething under the hegemony of the Hittites. And the moment they could, they broke free from their influence only to be reabsorbed into another empire. Actually, the whole of the northern Levant looks like a jar of scorpions busily trying to sting the other one to death before they were stung and killed first.

So, if we consider all the problems, revolts, wars, thefts, and murders that were taking place in this part of the world Rib-Hadda's problems fell solidly within the spectrum of middle-eastern politics, empire building and empire collapse. The difference is that Rib-Hadda was just the most vocal about them and spelled out in microscopic detail what they were. So, given these facts it becomes obvious that if Akhenaten had sent troops out to suppress every single revolt that was taking place in the provinces, he would have marched his army to death, ground his chariots into sawdust, and watched his horses die of thirst and starvation. And what would be the payoff? Nothing but more revolts, rebellions, and assassinations once the dust had settled after he left. No, all in all, it was better to let the frogs and the mice battle it out as long as they paid their tribute when it fell due and they didn't threaten the cat that was watching them.

In the past wars were conducted using bows and arrows, bronze knives, swords, and chariots. In the present age they're conducted with planes, rocket propelled grenades, tanks, sub-sonic, supersonic, hypersonic, and inter-continental ballistic missiles depending on the type of war being conducted. In other words, the territory stays the same, the only thing that changes are the players and the weapons. In short, middle eastern politics was a deadly game both in the past and in the present and undoubtedly into the far future.

Given this choice Akhenaten undoubtedly realized that if he fired Rib-Hadda he might replace him with somebody else who was even more incompetent, or like Abdi-Asirta more treacherous. This conjecture is supported by the fact that once the two men were dead and, in their graves, nothing changes for their successors; the never-ending war continues in the shadows of the great empires that surrounded them like the oceans that surround tiny islands.

All in all, Rib-Hadda didn't appear to be any better or worse than any other mayor in the Levant. However, the one thing that makes Rib-Hadda absolutely unique in Bronze age history is the fact that we have the undiluted, uncensored, and at times incredibly undiplomatic thoughts of one of the greatest minor league players in ancient history. We hear of his hopes, his tragedies, and his fears. We watch him grovel before the pharaoh in his letters, and then turn around in the same letter and demand immediate action. He can be tactless, petulant and whiny at times and exasperatingly repetitive at others. When Rib-Hadda can't get what he wants from the pharaoh he tries to circumvent him by getting other subordinates to plead his case for him.

Among other qualities that Rib-Hadda has, is that he is a courageous man who killed a would-be assassin after being stabbed nine times himself, and amazingly survived. He knew who his enemies were, and what they were capable of and took action to counter it.

On a more sinister note, when need be, he was also utterly ruthless selling his citizens into slavery in other towns for supplies, and crushing a revolt in Beirut by mercilessly killing the citizens who had turned into rebels.

Alas Rib-Hadda had all the qualities of a tragic character, his greatest strength, which was his loyalty, was paradoxically also his greatest weakness. For reasons that baffle me personally, he was absolutely loyal to a monarch who did in fact treat him like the dirt beneath his feet and didn't lift a finger to save his life or prevent him from being killed. Unfortunately, in both politics and real-life dirt has two purposes 1) to walk on, and 2) the other to bury your enemies in. And that is what the Pharaoh did to Rib-hadda; he treated him like dirt and then buried him in it when Rib-Hadda was murdered.

In closing I'm reminded of what the great Egyptologist James Henry Breasted once wrote of Akhenaten using an obsolete spelling of his name: "Until Ikhnaton the history of the world had been the irresistible drift of tradition. All men had been but drops of water in the great current. Ikhnaton was the first individual in history." In this case I have to respectfully disagree with the great Breasted. No, in my opinion the first individual in history, if such an exalted title can ever be given to just one person, is more appropriately given to Rib-Hadda an inconsequential nobody, who through a twist of fate became almost as well known as the King he served.

The End

Bibliography

Aldred, Cyril Akhenaten, King of Egypt

Beckman, Gary Hittite Diplomatic Texts

Bryce, Trevor Letters of the Great Kings of the Ancient Middle East. They Royal Correspondence of the Late Bronze Age.

The British Museum; The Tell el-Amarna tablets: in the British Museum; with autotype facsimiles

Cohen, Raymond and Westbrook, Raymond Amarna Diplomacy-The Beginnings of International Relations

Cooney, Kara The Good Kings; Absolute Power in Ancient Egypt and the Modern World

National Geographic Society

Elena Devecchi – Jana Mynářová – Gerfrid G.W. Müller Current Research in Cuneiform Palaeography 2

Proceedings of the Workshop organised at the 64ᵗʰ Rencontre Assyriologique Internationale, Innsbruck 2018

Dodson, Aidan Amarna Sunrise

- Amarna Sunset

Faulkner R.O. The Ancient Egyptian Pyramid Texts

Faulkner R.O. The Ancient Egyptian Coffin Texts vol III spells 788-1185

Faulkner Raymond O. A Concise Dictionary of Middle Egyptian

Faulkner Raymond O. The Egyptian Book of the Dead the Book of Going Forth by Day. The Complete Papyrus of Ani

Hoffman, Harry A. Jr. Hittite Myths

Moran, William The Amarna Letters

Murname, William J. Texts from the Amarna period.

Myantova, Jana Texts from the Northern Levant: The Paleography in Context.

Rainey, Anson F. Cannanite in the Amarna Tablets; A Linguistic Analysis of the Mixed Dialect Used by Scribes from Canaan. Volumes 1-4 Society of Biblical Literature.

Schiff, Stacy Cleopatra a Life.

Sasson, Jack M. From the Mari Archives an Anthology of Old Babylonian Letters. Eisenbraun

The Northern Cemeteries of Amarna Egypt Exploration Society

Verbrugghhe, Gerald and John M. Winkersham Berossos and Manetho Native Traditions in Ancient Mesopotamia and Egypt.

Watson, Traci for National Geographic news. Heretic Pharaoh Akhenaten's capital was no paradise for many adults and
children.

Youngblood Ronald F. The Amarna Correspondence of Rib-Haddi, Prince of Byblos (EA
68 — 96) Doctoral thesis.